"The most significant spiritual responsibility of any generation is the spiritual well-being of the generation that follows. In *Raising Disciples*, Natalie Frisk outlines how intentionality is the key to this task. May God find us faithful in living out and reproducing a form of discipleship that accurately reflects the likeness of Jesus."

—**Marv Penner**, executive director of the Coalition for Youth Ministry Excellence, from foreword

"In *Raising Disciples*, Natalie Frisk offers incredibly thoughtful, practical, and personal ways to not only help kids become disciples of Jesus but also examine our own lives as the adults responsible for helping those kids experience Jesus in a true and lasting way."

—**Tim Penner**, coauthor and illustrator of *T* 'lustrated Bible

"Parenting is one of those ir   so many more questions than ans   ,l, sports, or friends, there are ar   ances that parents navigate and don'   , *Disciples* will help you navigate the most im   ge you will face as a parent: the challenge of leading   _uild to their Savior."

—**Carey Nieuwhof**, founding pastor of Connexus Church and author of *Didn't See It Coming*

"The great commission starts at home! Thank you, Natalie, for writing this important book! Christian parents and the village that supports them now have a theologically rich and practical guide to helping their children become apprentices of Jesus."

—**Bruxy Cavey**, senior pastor at The Meeting House and author of *Reunion* and *The End of Religion*

"Whether you are a parent, a children's pastor, a volunteer, or just someone who cares deeply about the future of the church, *Raising Disciples* is a book you're going to want to read, thoroughly digest, and most importantly, put into practice."

—**Gregory Boyd**, founder and senior pastor of Woodland Hills Church and author of *Cross Vision*

"*Raising Disciples* is a breath of fresh air for parents. I love Natalie's practical approach to living an authentic faith that values the Bible, honors kids, and equips parents to boldly love Jesus. She helps parents understand the developmental stages of childhood and how Jesus is understood at each level. I'll be sharing this as a resource!"

—**Brenda L. Yoder**, speaker, licensed mental health counselor, educator, and author of *Fledge: Launching Your Kids without Losing Your Mind*

"This book offers a strategically impactful tactic to change the world. Shaping the next generation is not only what makes Natalie Frisk's heart beat faster—it's what will make real differences in the lives of our kids, inside and out. As a Christian leader and parent, I can't recommend this book more!"

—**Danielle Strickland**, author of *The Ultimate Exodus* and *The Zombie Gospel*

"Help! That's usually what I find myself saying—okay, maybe yelling—when it comes to figuring out ways I can bring faith alive in my children's hearts and minds. *Raising Disciples* is that answer to my SOS cry. Natalie Frisk creates a lifeline with helpful tips on how to parent in a Jesus-centered manner."

—**Maggie John**, host and senior executive producer of *100 Huntley Street*

"Natalie Frisk's book is so encouraging and equipping. I love the nonjudgmental tone of realizing that as parents, we're all humans doing the best we can, and of realizing our strengths and weaknesses are an important part of the journey. This book will not only guide; it will encourage and walk alongside your own journey."

—**Christy Wimber**, author, pastor, teacher, church planter, and television host

RAISING DISCIPLES

RAISING DISCIPLES

HOW TO MAKE FAITH MATTER FOR OUR KIDS

NATALIE FRISK

HERALD
PRESS

Harrisonburg, Virginia

Herald Press
PO Box 866, Harrisonburg, Virginia 22803
www.HeraldPress.com

Library of Congress Cataloging-in-Publication Data
Names: Frisk, Natalie, author.
Title: Raising disciples : how to make faith matter for our kids / Natalie
    Frisk.
Description: Harrisonburg, Virginia : Herald Press, [2019] | Includes
    bibliographical references.
Identifiers: LCCN 2019009872| ISBN 9781513802596 (hardcover : alk. paper) |
    ISBN 9781513802589 (pbk. : alk. paper) | ISBN 9781513802602 (ebk.)
Subjects: LCSH: Christian education of children.
Classification: LCC BV1475.3 .F76 2019 | DDC 268/.432--dc23 LC record
available at https://lccn.loc.gov/2019009872

RAISING DISCIPLES
© 2019 by Herald Press, Harrisonburg, Virginia 22803. 800-245-7894.
    All rights reserved.
Library of Congress Control Number: 2019009872
International Standard Book Number: 978-1-5138-0258-9 (paperback);
    978-1-5138-0259-6 (hardcover); 978-1-5138-0260-2 (ebook)
Printed in United States of America
Cover and interior design by Reuben Graham

Scripture quotations are taken from the *Holy Bible, New Living Translation*,
copyright ©1996, 2004, 2007, 2015 by Tyndale House Foundation. Used by
permission of Tyndale House Publishers, Inc., Carol Stream, Illinois 60188. All
rights reserved.

Scripture quotations marked (NIV) are taken from the Holy Bible, *New International Version*®, NIV®. Copyright © 1973, 1978, 1984, 2011 by Biblica, Inc.™
Used by permission of Zondervan. All rights reserved worldwide. www.zonder-
van.com The "NIV" and "New International Version" are trademarks registered
in the United States Patent and Trademark Office by Biblica, Inc.™

23 22 21 20 19   10 9 8 7 6 5 4 3 2 1

To my mom: thank you for raising this disciple.
To Sam: I am so glad we are in this together.
To Erin: "I'll love you forever. I'll like you for always.
As long as I'm living my baby you'll be."

CONTENTS

FOREWORD

The most significant spiritual responsibility of any generation is the spiritual well-being of the generation that follows. God's "plan A" for raising disciples is both taught and modeled throughout the pages of Scripture. In Psalm 78, the psalmist declares, "We will tell the next generation the praiseworthy deeds of the Lord. . . . He commanded our ancestors to teach their children, so the next generation would know them, even the children yet to be born, and they in turn would tell their children. Then they would put their trust in God and would not forget his deeds" (vv. 4-7 NIV). Clearly, there is both a sense of responsibility and joy in ensuring the next generation's understanding of who God is and how he interacts with his people. Near the end of his storied life, David passionately pleads, "Even when I am old and gray, do not forsake me, my God, till I declare your power to the next generation, your mighty acts to all who are to come" (Psalm 71:18 NIV).

The thing that strikes me about these passages is the purposeful intentionality with which generation-to-generation faith formation is embraced, and as you will read in the pages to follow, intentionality is the key to raising disciples.

What happens when that sense of spiritual purpose is lost? The answer to that question is found in one of the saddest verses in the Bible. It is a declaration that must break the heart of God and must motivate us as contemporary parents *to* pay close attention. A short reminder of the narrative leading up to this saddest of conclusions will reveal a pattern that can't be ignored.

After being freed from generations of Egyptian slavery, God's people wandered for forty years en route to the Promised Land God had prepared for them. When the time for them to enter the land of promise was imminent, Moses passionately reminded them of how important it would be for them to live with spiritual intentionality, and of the commitment to passing the faith to the next generation. The Jordan River miraculously opened, and God's people walked through on a dry riverbed to receive their inheritance.

As the last of the wanderers stepped into their promised future, Joshua (who had been given the responsibility to lead in Moses's absence) recognized the significance of what they had collectively experienced and sent twelve men back into the middle of the dry river. He commanded them to select twelve large boulders and erect a monument in the middle of their community. The purpose of this makeshift altar was so that "when your children ask" (Joshua 4:6 NIV), a teachable moment would be created, and God's strength and faithfulness would be affirmed in the retelling of the story.

That generation of parents saw God's unmistakable power on display over and over in the days to come. The toppled walls of Jericho; the unlikely victory over Ai; the lavish blessing of prosperity; the bright future that now was theirs. It was this same group of people before whom Joshua declared, "As for me and my household, we will serve the Lord" (Joshua 24:15 NIV). It was this same group of people who enthusiastically echoed Joshua's words committing to the same spiritual single-mindedness. But sadly, the story does not end well.

In Judges 2, we read these tragic words: "After that whole generation had been gathered to their ancestors, another generation grew up who knew neither the Lord nor what he had done for Israel." In just one generation, the most important thing had been lost. "They forsook the Lord, the God of their ancestors, who had brought them out of Egypt. They followed and worshiped various gods of the peoples around them" (vv. 10, 12 NIV).

Christian parenting is a great responsibility and a great privilege. God calls us to faithfully represent the gospel in every interaction we have with our children. And while there are no guarantees that we will see the outcome we hope and pray for; our role profoundly shapes us as we guide our children toward truth.

Scotty Smith, in his book *Everyday Prayers*, puts the spiritual responsibility of parenting into a beautiful and humbling perspective. He prompts his readers to pray, "You've called us to parent as an act of worship—to parent 'as unto you,' not as a way of saving face, making a name for ourselves, or proving our worthiness of your love. . . . Since our children and grandchildren are *your* inheritance, Father, teach us—teach me—how to care for them as humble stewards, not as anxious owners. More than anything else, show us how to parent and grandparent in a way that best reveals the unsearchable richness of Jesus in the gospel."[1]

Spiritually purposeful parents always begin with the end in mind. Assuming the desired outcome is children who are fully devoted followers of Jesus, let's commit to creating a relational environment in which the Holy Spirit is free to accomplish God's divine purposes in the lives of our children and grandchildren. Then they will be equipped to faithfully raise godly children when they are entrusted with the next generation.

We tend to raise up disciples after our own kind. In *Raising Disciples*, Natalie Frisk offers instruction and inspiration in the holy practice of discipling children and youth. May God find us faithful in living out, and then by God's grace, reproducing a form of discipleship that accurately reflects the likeness of Jesus.

—*Dr. Marv Penner*
Executive director of the Coalition
for Youth Ministry Excellence

INTRODUCTION

Hey there, mom, dad, uncle, aunt, neighbor, granddad, nana! Thanks for taking the time to pick up *Raising Disciples*. While I will often refer to parents throughout this book, please know that I mean you too, whoever you are: you as a biological parent, adoptive parent, or spiritual parent. While some of what I write will be most helpful for primary caregivers, much of this book will speak to anyone who is a spiritual parent: youth advisors, Sunday school teachers, mentors, pastors, aunts, uncles, grandparents, godparents, youth pastors . . . you get the idea. I really believe that whoever said that it takes a village to raise a child wasn't kidding. So if you're not a primary caregiver but you've engaged at a spiritual level with a young person, thanks for being part of someone's village. They will never forget it.

Perhaps you're on the fence about picking up this book, or you're just curious why you feel in your gut that this is a book you should read. Let me explain: while this book comes out of my life as a parent, it comes more predominantly from my experience as a youth pastor interacting in the area of family ministry throughout the years. This book is my attempt to answer all the questions that I have been asked about discipling kids, as well as some that haven't been asked that probably should. While there are many books on parenting and Christian parenting, I think there is a gap in the area of discipling our own children. We can talk about raising kids, with all the ages and stages of cognitive, socioemotional development, and that's just peachy, but I believe that leaves us with a major hole in our children's development. That hole would be their soul.

We need to talk about our children's spiritual development. For all too long now, I believe we have not taken our children's spiritual development as seriously as we have taken their, well, everything-else development: athletic, artistic, social, educational, and so on. Over the past few years, there have been a handful of studies conducted in the United States and Canada in regard to youth and young adults who have left the church. There have been panel discussions and conferences—some of which I have been a part of—about what we can do to remedy these problems. What usually emerges from these conversations is a call to parents to own their role in discipling their children—a call for parents to do something. What I haven't seen is the strategy—the *how*. This book is my best attempt at describing how to make faith matter for our kids.

Discipleship is not a linear course, and neither is parenting. This book is my invitation to you to more fully understand both. I hope that as we dive into this together, you are equipped and encouraged in the adventure of raising disciples.

JESUS-CENTERED PARENTING

When I talk about disciples, or discipling, or discipleship, it's probably wise that I define these things for us before we get too far so that we are all on the same page—both literally and metaphorically. When I speak of a *disciple*, I am referring to someone who says "Jesus is Lord" and who attempts to live in a way that shows that these words genuinely matter. A disciple is truly a learner or student of Christ. A disciple is discipled by Christ and those who are further along in their spiritual journey.

When I speak of *discipling*, then, I mean the act of making disciples. A disciple of Jesus is, by definition, a disciple-maker. A person who disciples others helps them discover the way of Jesus in a real-life, everyday kind of way. And the process of discipling is called *discipleship*. Discipleship cannot be confined to a course or a slot of time in the day. It is a 24/7 way of living. Discipleship means doing what the apostle Paul wrote, "Imitate me, just as I imitate Christ." In other words, follow me as I follow Jesus (1 Corinthians 11:1).

In this book, we are going to explore the idea of Jesus-centered parenting. Jesus-centered parenting is a way of thinking about our children and parenting that puts Jesus at the center of it all. It allows our children to grow up discovering Jesus as they journey through an increasingly difficult world. It helps us look to Jesus for clarity in all of life's choices. Jesus-centered parenting is us pointing our kids to Jesus at every turn. It encourages discipleship over everything else. While we won't be able to protect our kids from every speed bump or pitfall, we can set them up to have the very best opportunity to know, love, and serve Jesus. That's what I believe it looks like to raise a disciple.

As Christians, we are disciples who are being discipled as we seek to disciple others. (Say that five times fast!) While some contemporary parents claim that children should be raised without bias toward one belief over another, I would argue that all of us are being discipled into some way of living. Children who grow up in a family that are hardcore Green Bay Packers fans are being discipled in the way of becoming hardcore Green Bay Packers fans. They are being brought into the "worship experience" of Sunday football gatherings and taught the language of the Cheesehead Nation. Children raised in a home where there is a high value for art and culture will be taken to galleries and museums. They will be taught to recognize van Gogh, Kahlo, and O'Keeffe. They will be discipled in the way of music and art, learn to sit quietly through lengthy concerts, and discuss the arts in a way that is most certainly cultivated by their parents. I'm not saying that either of these examples are necessarily antithetical to raising children in the way of Jesus. I'm just saying that as parents, we all disciple our children into various loves and loyalties. Why wouldn't we want to disciple our kids in the way of Jesus?

So in this book we are going to reflect on how and why it is important to create space for spiritual development for our children; discuss how to be intentional but not legalistic with our spiritual practices; and discover how to show and tell our kids about our faith in Jesus in a way that is meaningful to them.

I also want to give you a picture of what this book isn't (because unmet expectations are the worst!). This isn't a book about how to discipline your kids. It won't tell you what to say to your kids about sex or when they should wear deodorant (but, well: sooner is better). It won't help you discern when to start chores, or how to make sure your kids don't delay bedtime each night with their list of one hundred things that they need before sleeping. While I most definitely have thoughts on all those things, that's not the direction we are headed. That being said, I do hope that the heart of this book will help you in how you approach these topics and many others like them.

NOTHING LINEAR ABOUT DISCIPLESHIP—OR PARENTING

I have spent the entirety of my adult life reading about, writing about, and living out how to teach kids and youth about Jesus, the Bible, and all things Christian. After graduating with a degree in English literature from a Christian liberal arts university, I stumbled into a job as a substitute teacher at a Christian elementary school for a few months, and then took on a role at a Christian high school as an educational assistant supporting a young man with autism. I also taught ninth-grade French, and at the same time, I was an assistant coach for the women's basketball team at my alma mater and a coach for the varsity girls' basketball team at the high school.

Partway through those assignments, I realized two things: I loved journeying with and supporting students in their walk with Jesus, and I didn't really love the classroom. About that time a college friend emailed to tell me that the multisite church I was attending was hiring in youth ministry. He believed I would be ideal for the role. And as God laid down one bread crumb at a time for me, I followed. The church was The Meeting House: a multisite Anabaptist church located near Toronto, and I soon entered into youth ministry. To clarify, I should say that I entered into *full-time, paid* youth ministry, because I had truly gotten my start in youth ministry when I was in tenth grade. As a small group leader for middle schoolers, I learned a lot about discipling kids and cheering on their growth.

In 2011, after I had spent a few years in full-time youth ministry, my husband, Sam, and I gave birth to a sweet baby girl we named Erin. And all the thoughts and ideas about how to disciple kids became so much more real to me. I wasn't just supporting other parents discipling their kids; I, along with Sam, was now in charge of discipling our very own child. Things I had theorized about and suggested to other parents were now being put to their greatest test yet.

After my daughter was born, I had a very humbling experience. I recognized the great need to ask more questions to people who are much wiser than myself. It wasn't really until my daughter was born that I truly appreciated my own mother. My mom was my primary discipler, and I didn't acknowledge the depth of that until I reached parenthood myself. My mother also happens to have worked as an early childhood educator for more than forty years. So as a new mom, I frequently asked her questions about the things I didn't know, or about the things I didn't understand, or even about things in my own upbringing that I didn't like. I read parenting books, and stared at statistics, and dug into conversations.

I said it earlier, and I want to say it again: Discipleship is not a linear course, and neither is parenting. As disciples, we ebb and flow in our journey with Jesus. We may grow in leaps and bounds. We may lean closer and closer to Jesus, but then we may stumble and fall. We get back up, but it takes time. We may circle back as we recover from the stumble. Parenting is similar. As our kids grow, we ebb and flow in our parenting relationship too. We aren't always certain how to be what we need to be. We aren't always certain how to point our kids to Jesus. The reality is that sometimes we can be very good parents, and sometimes we are simply good enough parents. And sometimes that is just fine. Life doesn't always provide smooth terrain for us. We have to be flexible and work with what we have at any given time. We must be prepared to journey that terrain and not give up when we grow weary. And even though the course is not linear, I can't help but think that life would be boring if it were. I love a good plot twist, and I have already seen quite a few of them in my life.

I should mention here that just a couple of years before my foray into parenting, I began studying for a master's degree while working full-time in youth ministry. Needless to say, my studies became a hobby more than a focus, and it took me almost ten years to complete my degree. But I did, finally earning my master's in theological studies with a biblical study focus in the spring of 2018. About halfway through studying for that degree and being a mom to a preschooler while working in the busyness of youth ministry, I had a bit of a divine appointment. Since childhood, I have been a writer. In fact, in those childhood memory books in which some parents track their children's special moments, I had written down a goal each year from first grade onward: "When I grow up, I want to be an author." Some years I had written down additional ambitions: Olympian and teacher, for example. Author, however, was always first.

With that goal noodling around inside me since childhood, I was prepared for this question long before it was asked. I was approached by colleagues who were doing research on

~~DON'T~~ TRY THIS AT HOME

- What are you hoping to learn or experience from reading this book?
- When you hear the term *Jesus-centered parenting*, what ideas, thoughts, or questions come to mind?

1

THE MOST IMPORTANT THING

You rarely have time for everything you want in this life, so you need to make choices. And hopefully your choices can come from a deep sense of who you are.
—Mr. Rogers

Kids have the uncanny ability to get personal with people quickly. I'm going to attempt that leap here and now, and I hope I can pull it off. I want to ask you a question about your own life, and I'd like you to try to answer it honestly. I know I'm asking a lot, since we've really just met, but here it is: What is the most important thing in life?

I'm not trying to trick you, I promise. But I do want you to consider not just what you *think* or *say* is the most important thing, but what you actually *live out* as the most important thing. Sometimes we articulate one set of values and live out an entirely different set. If you're unsure of what I mean, take a look at your schedule. What occupies the most time?

What takes priority? What are you willing to cancel other things for? What do you look forward to the most? Is this the same thing that you say you'd value over everything else?

These may seem like rapid-fire, heavy questions, but we need to think clearly about our own lives and habits. At least I know I do. Even as I write this, I can see how certain things that occupy my day aren't really things I'd say I value. Yet there I go, checking silly newsfeeds and binge-watching shows on Netflix. That's my hypocrisy gap. I *say* I value people, relationships, and discipleship—but on my day off, I'd rather cling to a screen. I'm on this journey too, trust me—I so desperately need to practice what I preach.

When it comes to parenting, we all have our own hypocrisy gaps. We *say* we value a certain kind of parenting, even as we act another way. I know that can be painful to consider, but please know that I feel the twinge of it myself.

The great majority of parents—you and me included—have the very best motives when it comes to raising our kids. So as I say everything else that I'm about to say, know that the undercurrent of all this is: I think your heart is steered in the right direction. I am working with the assumption that you are doing your very best, because I really do believe we all are doing just that. I also want to make a deal with you that will, henceforth, be known as "the guilt trip clause." This book is not about feeling guilty, so please, let's not turn it into that. If you are reading along in these chapters and feel guilt creeping in, shut it down: either the guilt or the book. Take the guilt to Jesus and work that out, and then hopefully come back to the book later.

There is so much parental guilt these days, and in no way do I want to contribute to it. I find parental guilt creeping in on me so often that I'm embarrassed to admit it. When I see a kid who is more athletically, academically, or musically advanced than my own, I think, "Oh no! Is my daughter behind? I need to help her work on [fill in the blank with the appropriate area of deficit]." *Guilt.* When my daughter is unkind or rude to other people? *Guilt.* When I am away or am unable to spend time with her for a few days? *Guilt.* When I give her too much screen time simply to occupy her because I am busy? *Guilt.* When I assume something instead of listening to her talk? *Guilt.*

Honestly, most days I have dozens of flashes of such guilt—and that is without anyone pointing out my flaws to me! When that happens, I fall down a guilt well so deep that I need quite the team with rope and harness to help me out. We all experience more than enough parental guilt, from every angle, that we simply do not need to add to one another's load. And so, let's now officially place the guilt trip clause into effect. If *Raising Disciples* is prompting an excess of guilt on your part, put it down. Come back later. (Please come back later! I'll miss you.)

REPETITION MATTERS

As we begin this journey, I want to plant us in some solid biblical soil. In the Old Testament book of Deuteronomy, Moses belts out instructions to the Israelite people. While these words were uttered thousands of years ago, the lesson for us today is just as great as it was for his listeners:

> Listen, O Israel! The Lord is our God, the Lord alone. And you must love the Lord your God with all your heart, all your soul, and all your strength. And you must commit yourselves wholeheartedly to these commands that

I am giving you today. Repeat them again and again to your children. Talk about them when you are at home and when you are on the road, when you are going to bed and when you are getting up. Tie them to your hands and wear them on your forehead as reminders. Write them on the doorposts of your house and on your gates. (Deuteronomy 6:4-9)

I'm told this Bible passage is a must-have in every book about Christian parenting. And while I'm not exactly a sucker for tradition, the truth is that this passage is packed with parenting wisdom for us today. Although I'm not a huge fan of taking parenting advice from the Old Testament—what with the stoning of disobedient children and all—I do think there are some glorious nuggets in there. Including this one.

Moses is in the middle of an oration to the Hebrew people about decrees and regulations, and he throws in the phrase "Listen, O Israel! The Lord is our God, the Lord alone." This is called the Shema and is used in regular Hebrew prayers and, today, in Jewish prayer services. It would have also been a clear phrase to indicate to all of Moses's listeners that they had better listen up, because here come some of the most important commands ever: "Love the Lord your God with all your heart, all your soul, and all your strength."

If we were able to simply focus on this, we would be phenomenal parents. We would be incredible role models to our children, and we would be focused on living a Jesus-centered life. Yet this passage offers us some additional, very practical parenting advice.

We are to commit ourselves to these commands—given by Moses but truly unveiled by Jesus—to love God and love others. The commands, or the law, for the Hebrew people were the terms of the covenant that they had with God. We now live under the new covenant—the one initiated by Christ himself. That means we live in a new way, focusing less on the commands themselves and more completely on Jesus. As the writer of Hebrews says, "When God speaks of a 'new' covenant, it means he has made the first one obsolete. It is now out of date and will soon disappear" (Hebrews 8:13). This new covenant was introduced and made possible in Jesus at the Last Supper, when he held up his cup after dinner and said, "This cup is the new covenant between God and his people—an agreement confirmed with my blood" (Luke 22:20). As Paul explains in his second letter to the Corinthians, "The old written covenant ends in death; but under the new covenant, the Spirit gives life" (2 Corinthians 3:6). We are able to point our kids to the life-giving new covenant that is made possible in Jesus. And when it comes to the Deuteronomy passage, as Christ-followers we are able to take the sentiment of this verse and wholeheartedly commit to the new covenant.

Moses says to repeat the commands again and again to our children. In an illiterate or preliterate culture, such as the one in which Moses lived, verbal repetition was a vital tool for anyone seeking to hold on to information. Today, any early childhood educator will tell you that repetition is still one of the primary ways that children learn. That's why four-year-olds will ask you to read the same book sixteen times in a row. They are preliterate, and repetition is how they learn. Similarly, repeating the core message of Jesus to our children over and over again is how they will discover his great love for them.

Moses goes on to tell the people to "talk about [the commands] when you are at home and when you are on the road,

when you are going to bed and when you are getting up"
(Deuteronomy 6:7). There are so many amazing tidbits in
this verse:

1. Talk about them when you are at home
2. Talk about them when you are on the road
3. Talk about them when you are going to bed
4. Talk about them when you are getting up

Let's start with "at home." We've got to begin by talking
about Jesus at home. That's pretty much the heart of this
book. Raising disciples means that we talk about Jesus. A
lot! Talk about Jesus at home, show and tell about Jesus at
home, share about Jesus at home. Pastor and teacher Jessica
LaGrone writes, "Our family is our first church."[1] It's at home
that we first truly discover the body of Christ as a kind of
microcosm. We get to know who God is in a relational way
in our family. All the members of the family bring their own
gifts and their own ideas, and each views things in their own
way. In the family unit we learn to interact and value one
another for who each person is as a child of the Most High
God. As we talk about Jesus at home, our kids soon discover
that Jesus is someone we value, someone we love, and someone who matters a whole lot to us. In future chapters, we'll
delve into the nitty-gritty details of how to do this well, but
we'll just start with highlighting that this is of the utmost
importance (and stay tuned!).

Moses says that we should talk about the commands "on
the road." In Moses's day, a great deal of time would have
been spent on the road. Consider that the Israelites spent
forty years journeying in the wilderness, and that in that era
most travel was done by foot. That's a lot of road. Similarly,

today many of us spend a lot of our time on the road with our kids. Now, in truth that may look like a glorified taxi service, getting kids to and from various activities. Nonetheless, there is often ample "on the road" time for conversations about Jesus. Sometimes intentionally not turning on the radio, and thus creating idle time for thinking or talking, can be a gift to you and your child. As a parent, I find that the best conversations with my daughter happen in two places: in the car on a long journey and in bed as she is about to fall asleep.

This leads us to Moses's instruction to talk about loving God "when you are going to bed." There is something about the quiet and slowing of pace of bedtime that opens the door to deep conversation and unfiltered thinking. When I was a youth pastor, I looked up to a parent of three teens in my youth group. Her name is Sue. Sue had clearly done something right. Her three kids were terrific human beings: intelligent, kind, and Jesus-loving. I asked her once what her secret was. Because of a naturally baked-in humility, she laughed at my question. But then she gave me some of the best parenting advice I have ever received. Sue told me that when my husband and I buy a new bed for our daughter, we should buy a bed larger than she needs. She and her husband have done this for each of their kids, and most nights she spent time with each kid for a few minutes before bed, rehashing their days. She said that the absolute best conversations came during those times at night before sleep. Honest, vulnerable, and true conversations.

I was sold. So when it came time to buy our daughter a post-toddler bed, we bought one that was much too big for her. And each night, my husband and I have a bedtime routine that looks something like this: We pray, we sing a song, and then we lie beside our daughter for a few minutes, without an agenda. The prayer time is fairly consistent, but we flavor it up every now and then. We start with thanks. When Erin was quite young, I'd say, "Dear God, thank you for . . ." and she'd finish that thought with people, or random objects, or important parts of her day. Then I'd say, "God, please help . . ." and she'd fill in the blanks with the things she needed help with—for example, "help me not to be afraid in the night" or the things she knew other people needed help with. As she has grown older, I've also taken time to teach her the Lord's Prayer, so we will often pray that after this prayer. Then we sing a song. From the time she was about two and a half that song has been "I'll Love You Forever," from the Robert Munsch classic children's book *Love You Forever*. And to be sure we do it right, she ensures I rock her back and forth, back and forth, back and forth. Then we just lie there. She speaks, or she doesn't. She asks questions, or she doesn't. She makes incredibly mature statements, or she doesn't. This is a very regular, very consistent thing. It has made her feel safe and secure. It has given her great comfort. It has also shown her the love of Jesus in tangible ways. That bed has been the best financial investment we have ever made.

Ah yes, back to Moses. Moses also says to talk about the laws when we get up. I'm going to translate this for Christ-followers this way: let's talk about Jesus when we get up. My daughter leaps out of bed each morning as if small cartoon birds are going to dress her. She's up and ready for life. And so I want to be up and ready for her. I also want to help her begin her day on the right foot, and I'm pretty certain that "on the right foot" looks like a day that starts with Jesus.

But I'm not my best in the morning. I can fake it a little, but not much. I have a lot of friends, but the morning isn't one of them. I've always wished I could be like my mother, who spent a least half an hour in the Bible before us kids woke up in the morning. But that isn't me.

So I've embraced my own reality, and we've landed on a system that works. While my daughter is eating her breakfast, we typically read a portion of a daily Bible reading for children that she loves. This is our best attempt to "talk about it when we wake up." Of course, sometimes our mornings don't work out exactly as we hope. We sleep late, it takes longer than usual to make lunches, we can't find matching socks, or all the above. But when I get distracted by all these things, my daughter sometimes asks for the reading. It's a routine she now expects.

Moses's next instruction is "Tie them to your hands and wear them on your forehead as reminders. Write them on the doorposts of your house and on your gates" (Deuteronomy 6:8-9). Some Israelites took this quite literally and wore little boxes, with the commands written inside them, tied around their heads. Some had them written on their doorposts. Variations on these practices continue to this very day. While I'd like to joke about a misread metaphor, it's also true that many of my peers tattoo their favorite Bible verses on their bodies. So I can't say the practices are much different.

Tattooed or not, we who follow Christ recognize the importance of knowing Jesus inside and out. It is extremely helpful to have physical reminders of the good news message of Jesus around the house and in life. As a curriculum pastor, I consider it a win if children's artwork from Sunday morning ends up on the fridge, on a wall, or in a prominent place in the home. When families place a physical reminder of God's love around their homes, it matters. Some of my friends have Bible verses written on chalkboards in their kitchens. This is a fantastic way to highlight an aspect of God's beautiful story, or to help children (and adults alike!) learn key verses from Scripture. While we may smile at those Scripture wall hangings done in needlepoint by our grandmothers, I hear they are making a comeback. These are the kind of doorposts-and-gates moments that I champion now.

Throughout this book, we're going to dive more deeply into this idea of raising disciples. What does parenting look like when we do it through a Jesus-centered ethic? How do we talk about these things with our kids? How do we guide our kids into a faith that is lasting? How do we disciple our kids in the way of Jesus?

As we investigate these questions, I believe we'll find that Moses had some great starting blocks for building a solid foundation for spiritually parenting children, even thousands of years later. And it's one thing to simply read these thoughts and ideas, and another to really chew on them. To help you digest these thoughts, I will offer some (hopefully!) helpful questions at the end of each chapter. Reflecting on these questions will fuel ideas for living out this Jesus-centered parenting ethic and help you focus on the most important thing.

WHAT FILTERS DO WE USE?

Now let's think back to that question: What do you think is the most important thing in life? Reflect on your schedule, your priorities, and your experiences, and consider what that "most important thing" is for you. Maybe you realize, as you reflect, that you are not thrilled with what that thing appears to be. Well, my friend, today is a new day, and you have the opportunity to hit the reset button. Or maybe you are discovering that the most important thing really *does* feel like the most important thing. Fantastic! Well done, you! Then again, maybe you haven't quite had the proper coffee quota yet to answer such an introspective question. No problem. Just keep reading and brew those beans.

It may be easier to see what you value if I ask you a related question: What do you think is the most important thing for your child? I have a seven-year-old daughter, and as my husband and I make decisions on her behalf, we run every choice through several filters. Is this decision good for her? Is this activity healthy for her? Is this the commitment that's best for her socially and emotionally? (And sometimes: Is this going to tire her out adequately? Because, wow, does our kid have a lot of energy! We joke that she is the trinity of kids: three in one.) Whether we are conscious of it or not, we likely use our "best thing" or "most important" parenting filters when we make a decision for our kids.

We also don't make parenting decisions in a vacuum. We don't simply choose our own parenting filters (what is best, what is most important, what is healthiest) out of thin air. Surrounding us are parenting narratives, narratives of who we should be, what our primary concerns should be, and how we should raise our kids—narratives that are, often, completely contrary to the Christian narrative. The narrative to which I have committed my life is the story of Christ. It's a narrative that says "Jesus is Lord." And that means that Jesus is the most important thing; Jesus is the ruler, the king, the "boss" of my life. Jesus is the filter through which everything else goes for me and our family. There are different labels we can give this filter, but throughout this book I am going to call it a Jesus-centered approach. When Jesus is Lord, he's the center of our lives. Our lives can and *should* revolve around him.

When it comes to parenting, as well as other roles we fill, sometimes we need to hit the pause button and ask ourselves, What really *is* the most important thing? I need to do this almost daily. Some things we do because we think we have to. Some things we do because we think they are important. But many things we decide we don't have time to do actually *are* important, according to the Christian narrative.

Once again, I want to remind you of the guilt trip clause. This isn't about guilt, missed opportunities, or what you *should have* done. This is about living from this moment on with Jesus at the top of our priority list—with Jesus as the center of our lives. It's about living with all decisions, thoughts, and commitments flowing from a relationship with him. For me, Jesus is Lord: this is the most important thing. I want all my priorities and decisions to flow from Christ. Do they always? Nope. I'm a messy human. But this is what I aspire to, and I invite you to aspire with me. As a parent who says Jesus is Lord, I seek to parent from a Jesus-centered filter.

So can a Jesus-centered approach include sports, music, second languages, science clubs, and drum lines? Absolutely. But only if those activities help bring us closer to Jesus, and not if they are things that get in the way. When we live with the priority that "Jesus is Lord" in our lives and do our best to model that for our kids, we are giving them the very best. We are showing them the most important thing.

PACKED SCHEDULES

So what does it mean to choose Jesus as the most important thing? What does Jesus-centered parenting actually look like? I'm so glad you asked. We'll get there soon, but first let's take a look at some of the hurdles.

Friends and family sometimes recount their children's schedules to me, which often look a little like this: Mondays after school there are piano lessons. Tuesday after school it's gymnastics. Wednesday is swimming. Thursday, gymnastics once again. Friday is dance. Saturday is acting lessons. Sunday? Finally, after a busy week, here is a day to do nothing. School is a must. There are so many shoulds. And, well, God knows we love him, so he'll understand that we need a day of rest, right?

While I think God really does want us to have a day of rest in there, I also think that prioritizing our relationship with God is far more important than—dare I say it?—learning piano, gymnastics, swimming, dance, or drama. Now, there is nothing wrong with any of these activities; I believe each one of these activities can actually allow us to show glory to God and worship God in different ways. Yet if we allow them to, our activities and those of our kids can distract us from what is truly important. I realize that this could sound a little judgmental, and I ask you to forgive me for that. But busyness has become so normative in our culture that I don't think we have even begun to tally its many costs.

When I was picking up my daughter from her basketball practice, I overheard a conversation between a father and son. The son was also at basketball practice with my daughter, and his father was rushing to get him out of basketball as it ended because he had another activity immediately afterward. I heard the father say, "You can eat a little bit in the car on our way!" And the son, no more than six or seven years old, sighed heavily and said, "Dad, can't I just take a minute to read a book or something?"

My heart went out to him. He needed a break. He needed soul time. He needed spiritual development. We all do. In fact, as our kids develop emotionally, socially, cognitively, and so on, they are also developing spiritually. And this is an area that we cannot neglect, because it affects the whole of a person—especially a young person. In her book *The Spiritual Child*, Lisa Miller states that "without support and encouragement to keep developing that part of themselves, children's spiritual development weakens under pressure from a culture that constantly has them feeling judged and pressured to perform. . . . We're pressured to fill our downtime with productive activity, and we often feel compelled to fill in any quiet moment with diversions. This is how we live, and this is what we're modeling for our children."[2]

It isn't necessarily that we need to schedule soul time, although that'd be fantastic. The first step is to allow downtime to be just that—downtime—and to know that we don't have to stuff diversions or work into every free moment. When your children say, "I'm bored," you don't have to rush to save them from that boredom. It's out of the boredom of youth that amazing ideas and creative endeavors are born.

That being said, we do need to face the reality of the family schedule. When we make schedules for our families, we have many things to take into account. We often do it according to the musts and then the shoulds. I do this every month with our family schedule. You know what I mean: the kids *must* be in school, the kids *must* learn piano, the kids *should* play a sport, the kids *should* _____. You fill in your own blank. You know the track that runs in your own mind: there are so many musts and shoulds shoved into our headspace. The cultural narrative about what is best for children is so loud, and we don't want our kids to fall behind.

We can *should* ourselves to death. What I mean is that we train our minds to think about all the areas in which our kids *should* develop. Then, if they don't, we believe that we've epically failed. For example, my daughter *should* speak a second language. If not, I've failed. My son *should* learn an instrument. If not, how will he succeed in life? My children *should* play a sport. If they don't, how will they learn the valuable skills of teamwork and collaboration? My kid *should*, *should*, *should*. The shoulds become marching orders that we follow—prescriptions that we hope will reduce our fears. All these fears—of how our kids may fail, or of how we may fail them—creep in and influence how we make decisions. Fear becomes our default, an automatic posture that we no longer question. But let's ask ourselves why. Why is this or that activity on my schedule? Why do I have the priorities that I do?

Here's what I mean: our reasons for filling our kids' schedules are often good and well-intentioned. We sign our kids up for extracurriculars so that they become well-balanced students, learn important social skills, and develop a work ethic. All good things. We fill their days with activities so that they can thrive in school, get into a great postsecondary institution, and land that awesome and competitive career that ~~we~~ they have always wanted. Still good things. And once they've landed that, they won't have to struggle. They can find a partner if they want, get married if they'd like, have some kids (so that we can be grandparents!), and then they can be happy and successful.

There is nothing wrong with any of these things. But they are part of a cultural narrative that says safety, happiness, and success are the most important things. We want our kids to be happy. But the Christian narrative—the narrative in which I choose to live—is built around something much different from happiness. It's built on Jesus.

WHEN KIDS AND CHURCHES BECOME STRANGERS

During my years as a youth pastor, numerous parents of young teens came to me and said roughly the same thing. "I don't know why my kid isn't interested in or connected with the youth group at our church," they'd say. Or they'd ask, "Why doesn't our teenager want to come to church?"

Then, as I'd invite parents to tell me more about their children's experiences with church, I'd hear similar reflections: when their children were younger, Sunday mornings had been full of sports commitments. Their child had played a certain sport that was only offered on Sundays, and all their child's friends were playing, and they didn't want their kid to be left out. Or this sport was this kid's greatest skill or passion. And so it was obvious: their child had to play the sport. That sport or activity eventually progressed into a lifestyle. The team that was once a local recreation league and just for fun became competitive and required travel. Weeknights became practice nights, and weekends became filled with tournaments and games. Church attendance grew spottier.

And then, one day, the parent of a young teen would go to their youth pastor and ask why their child wasn't interested in youth group.

Now, trust me when I say that I know there are many complexities to this conversation. Why children, youth, and young adults stop attending church is a complicated and thoroughly researched topic. I am not suggesting that athletic commitments are the only factor which play into this, and I know that really great team experiences can be life-giving and can also provide other kinds of discipleship opportunities. But something stuck out to me in all these conversations I had with parents: that is, the young teen and the church community had become strangers to each other. How can you be interested in what you really don't know?

We will always act on what we prioritize. We spend time doing the things that we believe are most important. That leads me back to the initial question of this chapter, and the question that underlines every one of our motives: What is the most important thing in your life?

Let's consider our family's weekly schedules. We can assume that school and work are musts, but let's place everything else on the table. (Also, try to think about work in a nuanced way. There is a difference between the work that is a *must* and the work that is *excessive*; I know personally the potential damage that excessive work can do in my life and the lives of my family members.) So as we come to the end of this chapter, let's consider some questions together.

~~DON'T~~ TRY THIS AT HOME

- How do you see Moses's parenting wisdom already at play in your own family or the lives of families around you?
- What are the main time-occupiers in our schedules?

2

FINDING OUR ENOUGHNESS

You alone are enough. You have nothing to prove to anybody.
—Maya Angelou

My husband, daughter, and I were driving together recently when my husband pointed out someone riding a motorized skateboard. He and I were both surprised to see it, complete with lights that flashed multiple colors. My daughter looked at it without batting an eye and said, "Welcome to the future, Daddy."

In so many ways it really does seem like we live in "the future." I realize that isn't possible, because the future is always, well, the future. But what I mean is the future as I thought about it in my childhood: the heavily automated, *Jetsons*-style, everything-is-instant future. And while I realize I'm not flying on my commute each day (I wish!), it is safe to say we've leapt forward significantly during the past twenty years. The future is here, and it is fast, almost blurry. Disorienting maybe.

I often wish there was a pause button in life—not just because my daughter is growing up so quickly but because the world around us seems to be moving at an exponentially increasing rate. We have more, faster, clearer, smaller, quicker technology than ever before. According to Moore's law, posited by Silicon Valley pioneer and engineer Gordon Moore, the capacity for technological development by way of transistors on microchips doubles every two years. In other words, technology itself grows and changes at an alarming rate.[1] The narrative embedded in this technologically driven culture is that more is better, faster is better, and jam-packed schedules are better. Busy becomes a badge of honor that we wear proudly and shine whenever we get the opportunity. I just don't buy it.

Or do I? Shoot. Maybe I rent it at least for a while. Sometimes I get swept into the "busy is cool" or "busy means I'm important" type of mind-set. It becomes my mental mixtape for a while, and I sing it out as I fill my days with things that seem to make me important. But then God gives me a good shake, and I remember that is simply not true. Jesus lived a paced life: never hurrying, never rushing, never seeking busyness. In fact, Jesus even found time to pull away and reset. Mark 1:35 tells us that "Jesus got up and went out to an isolated place to pray." Jesus, the Son of God, paused for time with the Father, away from the distractions of daily life. And while I think this is so incredibly valuable for us as adults and parents, it is immensely valuable for our kids too.

In his book *Faithful Presence*, David Fitch writes:

> Our children are the casualties of a crazy, confusing, frenzied society. They are cast adrift from the moorings of their relationships at home, church, and in the neighborhood.

The world can't be trusted, they are told. We therefore need
certified programs for everything. Sports, music, tutoring,
dancing, the arts, boy scouts, girl scouts, and gaming must
all be programmed. . . . As the children shuffle from one
scrubbed program to another, their souls are pushed and
pulled, looking for the right path to direct their passions.
They are waiting to be drawn in to a place worthy of their
trust. They are longing to know and be known. The world
is obsessed with its children. Meanwhile the children want
presence. They yearn for face-to-face presence.[2]

What if we traded our own busyness, the weight of our
frenzied society, for a pace at which we can offer face-to-
face presence? What if we said no to the next offer of an
activity and just hung out with our kids? What if we said
no to one more opportunity for their musical or artistic or
athletic enrichment so that we can say yes to their spiritual enrichment?

I know it is a much greater challenge to live out these
commitments than to simply speak them. I am aware that
we live in a time and place in which the cultural narratives
compete with the Jesus-centered narrative in a problematic
and sometimes severe way. This is true in all areas of life,
but especially when it comes to parenting. There is so much
friction between the way of Jesus and the ways of the world.
Everywhere we look there is a message from culture that we
are not good enough, smart enough, wealthy enough, skilled
enough, or stable enough. Simply put, we hear that we are
not enough.

ALWAYS CONNECTED
But we want our kids to know and feel their enoughness.
And so, out of genuine parental love and hope, we *help* them.

We *push* them. We sign them up. We encourage them. We fill their schedules. We drive them to practices and rehearsals. We invest in their futures. And all the while, we want them to be safe. We want to know where they are and how they are when they aren't with us, and so we connect them with a smartphone.

Almost 25 percent of tweens and 67 percent of teens have their own smartphone. And while phones can be a helpful tool to stay connected, they can also be a major distraction and time suck. In fact, tweens who use a smartphone spend over three and a half hours per day on it, while teens who use a smartphone spend more than four and a half hours per day.[3] That's a lot of day. Phones add yet another layer to kids' piling schedules and the clutter that fills their minds. There is so much clutter.

While we're on the subject, let's take a closer look at some of those media usage statistics for kids and teens. Recent statistics show that the average North American child between the ages of zero and eight spends two hours and nineteen minutes using a screen per day.[4] Meanwhile, children between the ages of eight and twelve spend almost double that time.[5] And teens use over six and a half hours of screen time per day.[6] That's a quarter of a day! And while we live in the most connected time in history, we also live in the loneliest time in history. Screen time gives us the illusion of connection without the trueness of a physical, honest, and genuine connection that helps us grow and mature socially and emotionally. Our kids have constant contact but very little true connection. As a result, childhood rates of anxiety and other mental health issues are on the rise. We're not wired to be constantly wired.

ALWAYS STRIVING

The cultural narrative has us looking and asking for more, has us believing we need more, and we continue to sink more deeply into these painful cultural maladies. (And what do you benefit if you gain the whole world but lose your soul?) As our children pursue the plot points of the cultural narrative, they discover something painfully true: there isn't an end point. We'll never arrive. We are always, always striving. We cannot be who "they" tell us that we should be, because the markers of success keep changing. It's as if we are all riding a bus, standing without support. Adults know how to gauge the movement and stay on their feet, but most children will be knocked over at the first bump or turn. As we experience the pushing and pulling of culture against us, we adults have been able to prepare ourselves and get our footing. Our kids, however, haven't had the time to find their footing, and they can easily get knocked down without support.

As their parents or pastors or mentors or youth leaders, we can be that support. We are the ones who help them find their footing. And we do that by helping them be planted, rooted, secure in Christ. While the cultural narrative says, "You'll never be enough, have enough, or know enough," the Jesus-centered narrative says, "In Christ, you are enough." In Christ, you are whole. In Christ, you are complete. When we allow our children time and space to experience the power of this truth, our lifestyle transforms significantly. From striving to being in Christ. The very best gift we can give our children is to help them find their identity in Christ. Their *enoughness*. Their value as a child of the Most High God.

I suppose the practical next question is, How do we do this? If I cancel that next activity, won't my kids just find something on a screen to occupy them? Maybe. But I think this is where we, as parents, can really seize the day. We can swoop in to spend that time in face-to-face presence with our children. We can spend that time with our children on a walk, pointing out the beauty in God's creation. Or we can take teenagers to a coffee shop where they get to order something a little fancier than usual while we take a few moments to remind them of who they are in Christ. We can invite them into a spiritual practice. Or we can color a picture together or play Ping-Pong or watch them do a project, giving them time and space to be and to process their thoughts. We can listen: hear their questions, their random thoughts, and their weird jokes. We can be present so that our children can experience God's presence with us. And we can experience God's presence with them.

The whole world needs to take a deep breath. We need to know and experience the presence of God and the pace of Jesus. And while we might not have the capacity to make that happen by our own might, what we do know is that the world is made up of people's children. And each of us can help our children take that deep breath and lead them into the knowledge and experience of God. We can invite them to walk in the way and pace of Jesus.

In later chapters, we'll dig deeper into the how, but for now, I want to invite you into the pace of Jesus too. Take a breath with me, and experience God's goodness in this moment. I want you to know here and now in the very depth of your soul that in Christ, you are enough.

~~DON'T~~ TRY THIS AT HOME

- In what areas of your life do you feel inadequate?
- Do you have a "mental mixtape" about your own inadequacy? What messages does it send, and are they true?
- How are you being reminded of your own enoughness?
- How are you helping to make aware and remind your children of their enoughness?
- What are the things you can say no to so that your soul can breathe?

3

OUTSOURCING DISCIPLESHIP

Insecurity has been my lifelong thing.
—Beth Moore

Each Sunday, when my husband or I pick up our daughter from her class at church, we get something called a take-home card, which gives us the rundown of what was taught: Bible story, big idea, key verse, and a question or two to ask on the way home. It's true: as the curriculum pastor, I have written many of these. But I also really value them as a parent. In fact, if for some reason I don't receive this card on a Sunday, as an invested parent I will go back to the classroom and dig around until I find it. So will my husband. That card makes its way home with us and gets its own fifteen minutes of fame (or one week of prime location) on our fridge. We put it there as a reminder of what was taught, but also as a reminder of what we can continue to converse about with our daughter in the week. Moses has his doorposts and gates. We have our fridge.

I am so thankful for the leaders who teach my daughter each week at church. They are passionate and loving souls who desire to see kids come to know and love Jesus their whole lives through. I am thankful for their willingness to give their Sunday mornings to teaching, and for their energy and their preparation time. Did I mention their energy? I am thankful for their investment and for the role that they play in my daughter's life.

That being said, in no way do I think that my daughter's spiritual development starts and ends there. These amazing leaders absolutely play a role in my daughter's spiritual development—but so do my husband and I. In fact, my husband and I have many more hours per week with our daughter than her class leaders do. They have one hour on a Sunday. At best, that's fifty-two hours a year. At home, we have . . . well, a whole lot more than that. (If watching musicals has taught me anything, it's that we have 525,600 minutes each year.) So my husband and I must take seriously our roles to disciple our child.

The take-home card, and pieces like it, are useful tools in this discipling process. At The Meeting House we also have a parent blog, which provides additional ideas for connecting Sunday's teaching into the real lives of families. There are so many resources available to us as parents. Yet choice paralysis and information saturation make it difficult to actually utilize what is out there. Most of us are aware of the weight of responsibility to disciple our children, and we get nervous or uncertain about how to do what or even where to start. And of course, where do we find the time?

Let's call it like it is: many of us feel insecure in our own spiritual journeys. We don't think we pray enough, or read our Bibles enough, or encounter God frequently enough throughout our days. And truthfully, most Christian gatherings or teachings remind us that we are operating from a deficit. My hand is up for this one. Even though I'm the one literally writing the book on this, I feel this level of insecurity all the time. Whenever I hear someone share about their "quiet time with Jesus" in the mornings when they rise with the sun, I feel my insecurity growing in exponential ways. When I talk to someone with a rich prayer life where God speaks to them clearly in each moment of the day, my insecurity goes through a growth spurt. So it is safe to say that when it comes to leading our kids in their spiritual lives, the pressure is almost crippling.

While culture yells at us that we are not good enough—in how we live, what we own, how we parent, or how successful we are—the Christian world is yelling at us that we are not good enough spiritually. We don't read our Bibles enough. We don't pray long or hard enough. We don't give enough. We don't sing enough David Crowder . . . or whatever. While the truly Jesus-centered narrative says, "In Christ, you are enough," the narrative in Christendom—the dominant form of Christianity that loves power and privilege—is "Keep on striving." So it comes as no surprise that Christian parents begin to assume they don't have the skills or abilities to spiritually parent or disciple their own kids.

Whatever happened to that easy yoke that Jesus talks about? Where is that burden that is not heavy but light?

SUNDAY SCHOOL

Once upon a time, parents were seen as fully responsible for the spiritual development of their children. Christians, as part of a large church family, helped and supported, but parents were the primary disciplers of their children. There simply wasn't much of an option for someone else to take on that role. Whether that discipleship was truly in the way of Jesus is another question for another book. Still, parents discipled their kids in the way that they knew how: in the way of obedience to God.

A strange thing happened in the late eighteenth century: something called Sunday school began. But it wasn't what we know it to be today. Sunday school was literally a school *on* Sunday for impoverished children who worked the other six days of the week. The Sunday school was established so that disadvantaged children could learn the educational basics of reading, writing, and sometimes math while using the Bible as the primary textbook.[1] Over time, teachers realized that many important morals and values could be instilled in children during these lessons. What a novel idea! Many years passed, and the idea evolved. Sunday school eventually became more of what we know today: a time of Christian education and discipleship, in which adults school children in basic biblical truths.

This endeavor began as a beautiful example of the body of Christ at work in the world, meeting needs and sharing the gospel. Yet Sunday school also had an unfortunate byproduct: parents began to believe that the responsibility of discipling their own children could be shared more significantly. A slow but drastic shift had begun. Christian parents were beginning to allow others to take on the role of primary discipler in their children's lives. Parental discipleship shifted from an all-the-time thing to simply a get-them-to-church-on-a-Sunday thing.

I may be oversimplifying this. Yet it's not hard to see that, from the time of Moses's exhortations to parents to our modern-day scenario, the spiritual nurture of children has transformed. Simply put, a great number of Christian parents have offloaded the ownership of discipling their kids to Sunday school teachers. (Inserting reminder of guilt trip clause here.) None of this, I believe, is done with the intention to dismiss children's spirituality. But as we've done with a lot of other things related to our children, we've handed their discipleship over to the experts. But we are actually the experts in discipling our own children. In Christ, we really do have all that we need. We just need to be reminded and encouraged more often. So go, you! You can disciple your own child. You've got this.

YOUTH MINISTRY

I'd be remiss if I didn't mention another piece of the parental shift puzzle that was introduced in the late 1960s and early 1970s. Just as Sunday school did with education, this shift was another by-product of an incredibly well-intentioned effort: evangelism. In the 1940s and 1950s, parachurch organizations such as Young Life and Youth for Christ developed as attempts to reach non-Christian youth in their schools and communities.[2] An innovative idea—getting teens to evangelize their friends through large events and gatherings—soon morphed into Bible clubs, and then churches started to catch the vision. What was once a parachurch strategy was embraced by the church, and specialized ministry for youth entered into the mainstream. To reach kids, to win them back, and to engage them were the goals. The dawn of a new era began: youth ministry made its way into the evangelical church world.

Youth ministry really did—and still does—meet a large need in our churches and communities. Teenagers are a complicated breed. Their hormones are raging, physical changes of all kinds are happening at an exorbitant rate, and spiritual questions often come fast and furious and at the most random times. Having a spiritual mentor or a youth leader—someone who is not related to them—is incredibly important during this time. Yet with this new addition to church life, the responsibility and ownership of parents was, once again, shifted to another source: the youth pastor. And if the youth pastor isn't "doing their job," then the teenagers aren't being discipled well, right?

It's amazing how we've outsourced the discipleship of our kids in such well-meaning ways. We have established ministries for them that have truly become the best and the worst aspects of a changing discipleship experience.

OUTSOURCED DISCIPLESHIP

So here we are today: we have experts for everything. We want our kids to do well in music? We find them a music teacher. We want our kids to do well in sports? We sign them up for a league or a team or a development program. We want our kids to do well in academics? We pay for an additional tutor or afterschool program. We want our kids to grow spiritually? We hire children's ministers and youth pastors.

With the best of intentions, the average Christian family now subcontracts the discipling of children and teens to children's and youth pastors. While the professionalization of youth and children's ministry is entirely well-meaning and loving, there is also an unfortunate by-product: we as parents pull back on our own level of engagement and allow others to step up to the plate. We assume that when we take our kids to Sunday school, our children will learn something about God. When our teens amble off to youth group, we breathe a sigh of relief that they will learn about God. (And the truth is, we probably have many more expectations about our youth ministry than we do about our kids' ministry, but that's a tale for another time!) Because our lives are busy and packed with so much, we mentally check discipling off our lists. The "God box" gets a checkmark, and we move on.

This may not describe your life in any way, shape, or form. These are broad generalizations, and they may not describe your family at all. And while I point out these things, I also want to remind us of the guilt trip clause. It is difficult to both be reminded of our imperfections and not fall into the spiral of guilt or shame.

But rather than avoid the realities, I encourage us to step into the tension. We need to be aware: we as parents are the primary disciplers of our children. This is a mantle we will wear for many, many years. We need to own it. Jesus-centered parenting removes the "God box" from a weekly to-do list and puts Jesus at the center of it all. So instead of the mind-set that says, "Phew. We got our kids to church on a Sunday, check. All is well," our mind-set shifts to hold Jesus at the center of every action in our week. We partner with Sunday school teachers and children's pastors and youth pastors and leaders in our church. That way, discipleship that gets a spark of new teaching at church or youth group continues to be cultivated and digested at home. We disciple our kids in tandem with the committed workers and volunteers in our church community. One 2007 study by LifeWay Research demonstrated that older teens were more likely to remain in the church if they'd had mentoring investment from five adults from their church experience.[3] These relationships matter.

And so we link arms with the children's and youth ministry workers at our churches. We are a team that disciples our kids. And we own that. We make the move to link arms. We ask questions. We pray for their work, and ours. We collaborate in ways that are intentional and, yes, sometimes take time and work to cultivate. But this is worth it for the spiritual lives of our kids. This is worth it for their entire lives. This is worth it because this is how we raise disciples.

~~DON'T~~ TRY THIS AT HOME

- Who have been your own primary disciplers in the faith? If you haven't done so already, take some time to share with your children your experience of having these people in your life.
- Think about who plays an important role in your child's spiritual growth. What are some intentional ways that you can connect and collaborate with them?
- Invite a couple of your own close spiritual friends to pray specifically for your child throughout your child's life.

4

DOWN-IN-THE-DIRT DISCIPLING

Every child you encounter is a divine appointment.
—Wess Stafford

At one point in Matthew's gospel, Jesus' disciples come up to him and ask a pretty presumptuous question: "Who is the greatest in the Kingdom of Heaven?" (Matthew 18:1). I imagine at least one of them is smirking, thinking that it is *totally* him.

Jesus does something that must really shock them. He calls over a little child, plops that kid right in their midst, and says, "Unless you turn from your sins and become like little children, you will never get into the Kingdom of Heaven" (Matthew 18:3). Ouch. Not only are the disciples not on the top tiers of greatness in the kingdom, Jesus is saying, but kids are considered greater. And in that day, when children were generally viewed as terribly unimportant, that is a radical claim.

Jesus goes on to say that if anyone becomes as humble as a little child, they will be the greatest in the kingdom of heaven. In other words, *humility equals greatness*. The humility he is talking about is the bottommost level of humility. A humility so humble that you aren't even aware you're being humble. Little children have no awareness of what humility means, yet they model it to us exactly for that reason. And Jesus, the Word who became flesh, entered into this world in the most humble and vulnerable way: as a baby born into dirt-filled, dung-smelling circumstances. He came to us as a human who could feel pain and discomfort, and who even had to go through puberty. Our God experienced puberty. Let that sink in for a minute. If that's not humility, I don't know what is.

So what does it look like for us to live with a level of humility that ventures toward the way of Jesus in this manner? Toward childlike humility? To be honest, I don't completely know, but I think it looks like giving up things that we feel entitled to, living a life that is other centered, being playful, and not taking ourselves too seriously. It also comes with a healthy dose of awe and wonder at the world around us. I also think it looks like not assuming an adult-centric worldview. It means we take into account people of every age and stage in our daily lives.

With an attempt at childlike humility in tow, let's venture into the next part of the passage: "Anyone who welcomes a little child like this on my behalf is welcoming me" (Matthew 18:5). When I see small children, I usually get a little bit giddy inside. Their smiles, their giggles, their little sausage arms. Gah! They are just the best gifts from God. How would you welcome Jesus? I've thought about this before, many times. I just can't decide. A run-into-his-arms kind of hug? A weep-and-fall-at-his-feet moment? A wrap-around-his-neck-and-cling-for-too-long hug? And what would I say? Oh my goodness! All the things I would say. Or maybe I wouldn't. Maybe I'd be speechless. (And for me to say that is something. I live and die by words.)

Either way, I know what I *wouldn't* do. I wouldn't just say hi. I wouldn't simply pat him on the head or not even acknowledge his presence. And while I'm sure those things are obvious, I often see people do them to children: ignore, patronize, ignore some more. It actually breaks my heart when people don't even acknowledge children when they enter into a space. Why do we make children feel so invisible?

Now, I'm certainly not suggesting we fall at children's feet and weep. That'd just be weird. But I do wonder what would happen if we'd realize the significance of children in the kingdom. What would it look like to take seriously these words of Jesus: "Anyone who welcomes a little child like this on my behalf is welcoming me"? Unfortunately, in many adult settings, church included, children are treated as a distraction, as a problem to care for, something to brush aside, instead of as core to what is happening. We are a terribly adult-centric society. People aren't fully treated as people until they are adults. Children are seen as *people-in-waiting*.

Of course, I don't think that it'd be healthy for us to swing the pendulum all the way to the other side and become a child-centric culture. In fact, there is a great danger in the pendulum going in that direction. While there have been movements of child-centered parenting and adult-centered parenting (both of which have crashed and burned), we can see that the overemphasis on either side tips the scales. This is why Jesus-centered parenting is such an important way to operate. Child-centric ideology creates self-centered individuals, because they have been taught that the world revolves around them. In a similar fashion, as an adult-centric society, we assume that the world works for us in a certain way. We get priority as adults. As adults, we are able to access so many spaces that children cannot.

At most churches—mine included, although we're working on it—we focus our language, our methods, and our systems around adults. The "main service" is considered the one in which the adult teaching happens. We dismiss kids from this service to their own teaching times, which are equally valuable but are rarely seen as such. In announcements, we share about upcoming teaching series that are specifically about what the adults are experiencing and learning, not the children or youth. When a church budget is created for the upcoming fiscal year, the adult ministries are seen to first and given priority, while the children's and youth ministries budget lines take a backseat. When we have a Bible study or small group, we have to solve the "problem" of the care situation for the children.

Is this sounding familiar at all? (If not, hooray! You're a step ahead, but you are still a rare breed.) Unfortunately, adult-centricity rules the day in our culture, but I truly believe health will come to the church when we level the playing field and see everyone's spiritual journey as equally important. It will be messy, and we may even get dirty, but I believe we will see kids who love—and want to remain in—the church. I believe we will see youth thriving. I believe we will see young adults leading in unprecedented ways. But we need to see kids and youth as having important spiritual value. At present, our current cultural setting wants to wait until they are "grown up" to assign any true value.

But Jesus doesn't view kids that way. He sees the intrinsic value of children. We need to see this value in kids—not just the kids in our own family but all children. I know it can be easy to write them off or to see them as someone else's concern. And really, sometimes other people's children can be obnoxious—I totally understand! But the children and youth of our congregations aren't simply someone else's concern; they are a gift to us all. They are image-bearers of the Most High. They are our teachers, showing us what child-like humility and faith can look like and reminding us of the awe-inspiring beauty of creation. They prompt us toward wonder and play. They inherently understand the spiritual dimensions of the world—a view that adults often lack. We can learn so much from kids and youth. We can experience God's presence with them, because as we welcome them in Jesus' name, we welcome Christ. May we extend our arms to all children as we move through life.

MAMA BEAR MOMENT

This Matthew 18 passage about children ends on a harsh note. Jesus shifts in tone from loving to protective, but I believe he does this to emphasize the deep-rooted value of children and his heart for them to be treasured. Here are his words in verse 6: "But if you cause one of these little ones who trusts in me to fall into sin, it would be better for you to have a large millstone tied around your neck and be drowned in the depths of the sea."

Oof. In other words, "Don't mess with my kids." Jesus is like the ultimate mama bear in this moment. He wants us all to realize the weight of responsibility that we bear when it comes to children. I've joked that this final sentence in the passage has become my theme verse. I consider it often as I write curriculum for kids and youth. I honestly can't shake it from my mind. I wear it not as a mantle of fear but as one of responsibility. I consider how curriculum can be written so that children won't be confused or tempted to stumble in some way. I'd much prefer the weight of that responsibility to the weight of the millstone. That being said, I think that as people who love and care for kids, we do need to consider our decisions and actions through that lens. Are we creating barriers between our kids and God in some way? I don't think we need to hold this in a fearful way; we simply need to be conscious of the reality that we have incredible spiritual influence over our children.

A little while after this scenario, Jesus and his disciples journey from Galilee down to a place in Judea, just east of the Jordan River. (Can you imagine the step count of Jesus and his disciples?) Jesus is discussing with the Pharisees and others the law of Moses. While they are there, this is what happens: "Parents brought their children to Jesus so that he could lay his hands on them and pray for them. But the disciples scolded the parents for bothering him" (Matthew 19:13).

Now, I've always judged the disciples when I've read this. I've thought, "Come on, guys. You just heard Jesus say that children are the greatest in the kingdom. And now you do this?" But here's the truth: we have the whole story, more thorough and complete than the disciples knew, and we *still* do this. We still try to shuffle the kids away from Jesus. Many of us in the church have been guilty, at some point or another, of scolding parents just as the disciples did. We have hushed children—who are just being children—when they are disturbing the grownups during worship. We throw an irritated glare at parents when their babies are crying during the sermon. We have told kids and teens to save their questions for later (yet we never return to them), and we have pushed them off to something else while the grownups do the serious business of discipleship. And we don't just do this in a church gathering; we do this everywhere in our culture. We diminish kids: their feelings, their ideas, and their spiritual lives. But Jesus—did I mention he's just the best?—stops the disciples and says, "Let the children come to me. Don't stop them!" (Matthew 19:14). Jesus welcomes them into his presence. He makes time. He makes space. He raises the level of importance of children in his cultural setting.

And then he makes this astounding statement: "The Kingdom of Heaven belongs to those who are like these children" (v. 14). What does that mean? Wonder filled? Humble? Trusting? Hopeful? Playful? Uninhibited? Giggly? Sausage arms? Okay, so probably not the last few. But while we don't know exactly what Jesus means, we learn here an essential truth: the kingdom of heaven belongs to those like the little children. There is something about who kids are, and how they move through the world, that is close to the heart of God. Children connect with what God wants of all of us. I want to be present in the midst of kids so that I can better understand the heart of God.

I imagine Jesus stooping down to be at eye level with the kids. I imagine that at least one or both of his knees were in the dirt. We read that next, Jesus "placed his hands on their heads and blessed them before he left" (v. 15). A blessing directly from Jesus—how cool is that? I often wonder what became of these little children whom Jesus blessed. Are they the ones who grew up to be leaders in the church? Did they help carry the gospel to different places? What happens in the lives of children when they receive the love and attention of Christ? What does the blessing and presence of Jesus translate into in the life of a child?

I don't have a clear-cut answer, but that's what we are exploring together in this book. As children encounter Jesus in a genuine way, a foundation is set in them for the rest of their lives. As we depart from this story, I want to highlight the last few words. Jesus did this "before he left." Now, this is just my additional commentary to the story, but I can't help but think that after Jesus prayed for and blessed the children, there was nothing further to be done in that place. It was time to move on. Jesus had done the best he was going to do there: he had blessed the children. What could be greater?

KINGDOM FOOTPRINTS

With these two stories of Jesus and children in mind, I want you to consider your own spiritual life for a moment. Is there an encounter you've had with Jesus that you value? How do you express your journey with Jesus in your everyday life? In turn, how does your experience with Jesus influence your parenting? How does it influence how you care for, develop, and nurture your children and their spiritual journeys?

These are big questions, and they can be overwhelming. Maybe it helps to think of it like this: those of us who care about the environment have probably tried to gauge and then reduce our ecological footprint. We want our ecological footprint to be small so that we are caring for creation in the way God calls us to.

But what is our kingdom footprint? In other words, what impact do our lives have on others on behalf of Christ's kingdom? We want *that* type of footprint to be big. So how is our kingdom footprint reflected in the lives of our kids? When our kids see us caring for others or doing practical things to show the love of Christ, our kingdom footprint grows. When we, in the name of Jesus, take time for people whom others don't take time for, our kingdom footprint grows. When we make decisions based on the love of others instead of the love of self, our kingdom footprint grows. When we pray, "May your Kingdom come soon. May your will be done on earth, as it is in heaven" (Matthew 6:10), and then match our steps with that prayer, our kingdom footprint grows. As we take intentional steps to be bringers of the kingdom, we are helping to point our kids to Jesus with every step.

Many of us will practice soccer with our children or encourage them to trudge through their scales on the piano. But how do we inspire them toward spiritual development? What are the special moments of their faith that we want to help them make space for? These questions probably don't have simple answers. They may require that we sit with them for some time. In future chapters we will dig into some potential answers to these questions, but I want to plant the seed here so that you begin to consider the answers for your own child.

I asked my seven-year-old what I should tell parents about Jesus. She said, "Jesus is like our shepherd and we're the little lambs. We should always be with the shepherd." As we raise our kids to be fully functioning adults, we need to model for them what it looks like to spend time with the shepherd. We need to help them find their way to the shepherd so that they, too, can spend time with him. We can be the parents who bring our kids to Jesus for him to lay his hands on them and bless them.

When we take the posture that Jesus took toward children in Matthew 18 and 19—kneeling down at their level, looking them in the eye to let them sense and know their value—this is true getting-down-in-the-dirt discipling. Pursuing a Christ-like posture is Jesus-centered parenting. This is how we raise disciples. Let's do this together.

~~DON'T~~ TRY THIS AT HOME

- How could we, as parents, level the playing field and treat the spiritual development of children as equal to or even more important than our own? How could congregations and small groups do this?
- What's your kingdom footprint looking like? How are you showing and sharing the love of Jesus in the world around you?
- What's your posture toward your kids these days? Is a shift needed in your stance toward your child?

church." We did a lot of that, the standing and sitting. Like liturgical Jazzercise. I also went to the Presbyterian church for an afterschool program called COC (which stood for either Children of the Church or, as we'd joke, Children of the Corn—it's hard to be sure), Pathfinders Club, and also youth group—which, in truth, ran a little more like a committee meeting than anything else. Bless those Presbyterians, they loved their committees.

But Pentecostalism was in my mom's blood, with her father and grandfather both pastors, and her soul craved the Spirit-filled worship and stimulating preaching. I loved the Pentecostal services: part reality show, part genuine spiritual immersion. We would also go to the Pentecostal church for weeknight events: kids club, then junior high youth group, and finally youth group. With youth group came more opportunities to be in church: an extra prayer gathering or social event night.

Even with all these points of connection with the Pentecostals and the Presbyterians, my mom was also an active discipler of us as kids. Frankly, I ate it all up. I loved church. I still do. I know that I'm in a dwindling minority of people who can say that, but it's true. Most of my peers—friends who sat beside me in Sunday school or who raced against me in sword drills (more on those later)—rarely see the inside of a church today. In fact, according to a 2011 study of kids raised in evangelical churches in Canada, there is a steady decline in church attendance from childhood to teen years to young adulthood. Between childhood and young adulthood, attendance or church connection is cut by almost half.[1]

And believe it or not, evangelical churches have a much happier story in terms of retaining their youth than do most mainline Protestant and Catholic churches. The drop-off is steeper and much more significant in these two affiliations.[2] And while you may be from a country other than Canada, the reality is that the numbers won't be that much different where you live. If you're in the United Kingdom, the drop-off of young people still affiliated with churches may be even steeper. If you're in the United States, the decline is steady, but hasn't quite reached the same level. No matter where you live, you may be experiencing the reality of teens and young adults opting to seek their spiritual fill outside the church.

I've racked my brain to think back through my own church experience with my peers, trying to map out why I went one way and most of my friends went another. I haven't completely figured it out. But somehow, as a child and then as a teenager, I glimpsed that being a part of church life meant being part of something greater: the body of Christ. My early memories of Sunday school included a damp basement, those orange plastic chairs, the rotating church ladies who taught the classes, and the popcorn, apple juice, and Bible cartoon movie days (the best ever: I can still taste the Styrofoam cup and apple juice flavor combination). And of course, the Bible lessons.

Although my memory of what exactly was taught in those Bible lessons is a little blurry, I do remember a very clear theme: Don't do this. Do this. Don't do this. Do this. Don't do this. Don't do this. Don't do this. A good girl does this. A good girl doesn't do this. God wants us to be good little girls and boys. The good go to heaven. The bad burn in hell. Every question had a clear right or wrong. Moral lines were drawn with a thick permanent marker.

That theme is a clue to the reason many of my peers haven't stuck around in church. Morality-centered teachings, which focus on the *what* of Christian discipleship rather than the *why*, are bound to leave many young people with the sense that church wants to control their behavior. The rigid boundaries set in their childhood don't seem to translate into their everyday lives as young adults, and so they toss the baby out with the bathwater. Goodbye, church! Hello, spirituality of my choosing.

What if we joyfully told our children about the *why*— following Jesus—rather than obsessing over the *what*? What if our children heard the gospel's call on their lives as one that focuses on Jesus and the fact that Jesus wants every action to be for him? What if instead of saying, "Do this, don't do that," we said, "Jesus wants what is very best for us. Jesus wants us to be the best version of ourselves, and Jesus wants us to follow him and his way"?

When we talk about Jesus, we talk about the good news. We speak of love, and sacrifice, and compassion, and enemy love. Our conversation revolves around the Jesus center, which is a love ethic. In love, we point our kids to Jesus again, and again, and again. We model forgiveness. We model kindness. We model patience. That's Jesus-centered parenting. When we talk about the shoulds and the shouldn'ts and the dos and don'ts, we give our kids a fear-driven message. That's morality-centered parenting.

Let's look at a morality-centered approach first, and then we'll consider what a Jesus-centered perspective looks like.

A MORALITY-CENTERED FAITH

When I was growing up, the *what* (moral behavior) rather than the *why* (Jesus) became the gospel itself. In fact, I am pretty certain that Christian parents of that era were discipled by the church to work hard at raising moral kids. "Bible-based parenting" was the big thing—which, frankly, is a scary concept when you think about the biblical recommendation for what to do with rebellious children (see Deuteronomy 21:18-21). I learned to do right and not to do wrong. I learned how to behave. I learned to be a moral person.

And trust me, I was so very moral—which isn't a horrible thing, and is something for which I'm grateful. But even morality can go off the rails. I was fearfully moral. For months after seeing the 1972 rapture film *A Thief in the Night*, I would lie awake in fear. What unrepentant sin did I have? What accidental trespass had I committed? Where was I missing the narrow path? The moral weights piled high, and they became a load I really couldn't lift. I knew Jesus loved me, but that only seemed to go so far. I thought I really had to be good to be "in" with certainty.

To hammer into our children the importance of being good, we teach children the Ten Commandments. We teach them a list of don'ts. And while it is helpful to guide children to understand what not to do, it is so important to help them understand the *why* behind all of that. If we look to Jesus and his call to love God and love our neighbor as ourselves, it becomes redundant to say, "Don't steal." Because if you are loving someone as you love yourself, you would never steal from them.

Allow me to elaborate by looking at an example of a morality-centered approach to Scripture. Let's say we are teaching the story of Ruth to a bunch of kids. A morality-centered approach looks something like this: "Be kind." Kindness is a great moral, so we teach the lesson of Ruth and Naomi and talk about Ruth's kindness. She was so kind! She could have left Naomi, gone home, and reset her life without too much hardship. But instead she clings to Naomi, won't let her go, and struggles to find the place where she and Naomi can glean enough food to survive until they encounter a rescuer. Their rescuer was Boaz—oh, his kindness to both Ruth and Naomi was so wonderful too.

As teachers and parents, then, we highlight Ruth's and Boaz's kindness, and we tell our children that we can all be kind, as Ruth and Boaz were. Be kind like Ruth, we say, because that's the good thing to do. What a great moral lesson! It truly is—don't think that I'm saying that being kind isn't important, or that teaching morals isn't a good thing.

But here's the thing: morals aren't transformative. Morals aren't what cause us to hold on to our faith during the storms of life. Morals become an impersonal, rigid list of dos and don'ts. Trying to follow a list of morals means that we are bound to fail, again and again.

A JESUS-CENTERED FAITH

Let's reset. This time, with the Ruth passage, let's try to place Jesus, not morality, at the center. So this time, as we consider telling the story of Ruth and Naomi to a group of young people, let's imagine how it would sound if Jesus were at the center of the story and our lives.

Side note: Perhaps you're thinking, Wait! Jesus wasn't yet born into the world—why take this view of the story of Ruth? Great question. Before the birth of Jesus, we would look to Ruth as a morality lesson and part of the historical narrative of Israel. But from the birth of Jesus, his life, death, and resurrection, everything is changed. In John 5:39, Jesus tells a group of Jewish leaders that all of Scripture points to him. Jesus is what the larger narrative, the story, is about. And with that, we look at the story of Ruth.

You see, Ruth was from a different country and people group than Naomi was. Ruth was what we would call a Gentile—that is, a non-Jewish person. Naomi was an Israelite. If I were teaching kids at this moment, I would say that Naomi was from God's special family and Ruth was not. However, because of God's great love for all people, God brought Ruth into his family—just as God brings you and me into his family.

For Naomi and Ruth, life was very difficult, and they struggled to get enough to survive. And Israel, throughout their history, struggled. In fact, the name Israel means "wrestles with God" or "struggles with God." And while Ruth and Naomi struggled, they trusted in God. Ruth found a field to work in, gleaning enough grain to provide food for herself and Naomi. And Naomi looked out for the both of them with her great wisdom.

In the meantime, their kinsman redeemer—that is, the guy who, in that era, was responsible for the women after the deaths of their husbands, as required by God's law—just happened to be the owner of the fields where Ruth had been gleaning. The kinsman redeemer was Boaz. He modeled great kindness in how he interacted with Ruth. In her time gleaning from his fields, Ruth showed Boaz that she was an incredibly hard worker. In keeping the law, Boaz married Ruth and provided a place for Naomi as well. The cherry on top is that Ruth and Boaz became the great-grandparents of David, and that means they are in the line of Jesus!

Yes, kindness is displayed. But what is more exciting in this story is the way it points to the unbelievable story of redemption in Jesus. Ruth represents all of us who are not part of God's special family. We get to be adopted into God's family, clinging to the promises to the Israelites the way Ruth clung to Naomi. And we get to let go and be redeemed through Jesus. We are saved. We don't need to struggle any longer. We are rescued from death, sin, loneliness, and so much more through Christ. We are brought to life, forgiveness, and family.

That's a much better story. Being redeemed from fear and from death and from sin is a much more exciting and compelling way to experience this story than being kind and good. Don't get me wrong: of course we should encourage our kids to be kind. Each morning, I pray with my daughter to be kind and loving even when it's hard—because that's what Jesus did and that's how we follow him well. Kindness is a fruit of the Spirit into which we encourage our kids to grow. But we need them to get swept up into the beautiful story of God. We need them to get drawn into this amazing story of rescue and redemption. There is transformation happening. That's the glory of the story: Jesus. That's the Jesus-centered ethic. Do you see the difference?

Then, as we speak to our children and use a Jesus-centered love as our delivery point, our expression of what we do and how we live changes. Our parenting and our teaching and our mentoring emerge from a framework of Jesus' love instead of from a finger-wagging, brow-furrowing list of dos and don'ts.

WHAT'S THE MOST IMPORTANT THING AGAIN?

It's time to remind ourselves of what our "most important thing" is as followers of Jesus who are parenting children. If our aim is to raise good, moral citizens, then morality-centered parenting works just fine. But if encountering and following Jesus is our most important aim for ourselves and our deepest hope for our children, then we may need to change directions. If "Jesus is Lord" is the most important thing, we may need to begin saying and living that, clearly and repetitively—because this is how children learn.

And we may need to be open to expanding our understanding of the good news of Jesus. Many parents and pastors and Sunday school teachers are good at telling kids they need to accept Jesus as their Savior. We've got that part down. Growing up, I knew that Jesus was my Savior. And though I might not have fully understood it, I knew that Jesus died on the cross for my sins. In fact, that was my default answer for every Bible-based question until I was about eight years old. Many times that was the right answer.

But I wish I had learned the fullness of the gospel message: that Jesus wants to be Lord of our lives, in the everyday sense, the every-moment sense. I wish I had learned that Jesus came to show us God's love—God's beautiful, perfect, gracious, willing-to-die-for-me kind of love. I wish I had learned that Jesus came to set up God's kingdom, and that being a Christian wasn't about earning a get-out-of-jail-free card but rather meant a fuller life now.

I wish I had learned that God's story was one long narrative that started with the creation of the world, extended throughout the Old and New Testaments, and that the story is not yet finished. I wish I had learned that I am a part of the same church that the people in Acts were a part of, and that, as a member of the church and the kingdom of God, I have a part to play in God's story. I wish I would have learned that when Jesus went back into heaven, he sent the Holy Spirit to come and help us, guide us, and be with us to do big kingdom work. This good news of Jesus—well, it's more exciting than "Do this" and "Don't do this," isn't it?

So what does all of this translate into for our kids? What do I say to my daughter tonight at dinner that will help her grasp this? What can you say to your son before school, or to your Sunday school class tomorrow, or to your youth group on Wednesday night, that will help them grasp the most important thing rather than settling for moralism?

I genuinely believe that helping our kids, at every age, see Jesus, know Jesus, experience Jesus, love Jesus, and follow Jesus is the most important thing. As parents and spiritual leaders, we can change the narrative for our kids. We can help our kids experience a Jesus-centered way of being. We can frame all they need to know about living as a Christ-follower by understanding God's great story. We can offer them Jesus as the thread that weaves it all together.

Yes, we can still take our kids to church three or four times a week. Why not? But we need to frame our spiritual conversations with our kids as being about Jesus rather than rules, traditions, or morals. Do we still sometimes say, "Don't do this" or "Do that"? Sure. But mostly we orient kids toward Jesus and his love ethic so that they can understand the *why* behind all the dos and don'ts. When Jesus is at the core, the morals will be natural by-products. When Jesus is at the center of our experiences and our conversations with our children, our children begin to see the life of faith as a life of joy and freedom rather than a life of trying and failing to meet standards.

~~DON'T~~ TRY THIS AT HOME

- If you grew up in the church, what are the sound bites or ideas that you remember most about Jesus, the church, or Christianity?
- What moral imperatives were taught to you as a child and teenager? Did you question any of these? If so, how?
- In what way does placing Jesus at the center of the conversation change your mind-set and the conversations that you might have with your children?
- Consider your favorite Bible story (maybe it is Jonah, or Shadrach, Meshach, and Abednego, or Deborah). What is the morality-centered telling of that story? What would a Jesus-centered way of telling it sound like?

6

IT GOES WITHOUT SAYING

Don't forget to breathe!
—Becky Frisk

At about age ten, I got The Talk. Yes, it was as awkward as you can imagine. After school one day, my mom invited me into the living room. We never sat in the living room, so I was already on to her. The living room had a sliding wooden door that clapped shut. The moment that it shut, the door rattled a little, like a low rumble of thunder. That sound announced to everyone in the house that someone was having a private conversation in the living room. We never shut this door except for conversations like this one. I knew what was coming, and I'm sure my face already flushed red with embarrassment before the conversation began.

My mom sat down beside me. She was noticeably nervous and embarrassed. The pitch in her voice had heightened ever so slightly. She told me she had something to give me, and she presented me with a book. It was a book on puberty, how the body works, and other things that cause ten-year-old girls death by embarrassment. It came complete with diagrams and drawings of all the reproductive parts. My face burned hotter. My mom flipped through the pages for me and provided commentary throughout the book. Bless her heart, she spelled out *s-e-x* instead of saying the word. Because we were just that kind of family.

Many adults feel just as awkward talking to their kids about Jesus as they do talking to their kids about sex. It's true: the awkward scenario that I've described is the scenario many children and youth encounter when parents talk to them about Jesus or faith. Parents' pitch changes, and they awkwardly fumble for a satisfactory answer to a question. Or they give their kids a book, providing commentary laced with their own baggage or assumptions, because they don't feel confident in what they are saying. Even worse, they may quote Bible verses out of context as their voice launches into preacher mode. Discussing dos and don'ts: no problem! Discussing God, faith, big life questions of meaning: these are sweat-inducing, panic-dripping parental moments.

Christian parents' inability to talk naturally about faith often has to do with a discomfort about their own spiritual walk. Some of us simply lack confidence in our own ability to talk about Jesus in general. Either way, it's an integration issue. In many families, Jesus is becoming an infrequent point of conversation—typically sequestered to appropriate discussion zones at church and a few minutes after the service. In a culture that has moved on from Christianity, our ability to talk about Jesus has too. We've lost the words to dialogue or share about Jesus in a meaningful way. By this, I don't mean we've stopped using words like *sancti-fication* or *justification*—those are great concepts, but not the point here. What I mean is that we've lost the ability to simply talk, day to day, with family and friends about what God is doing in our lives, or how the Holy Spirit is prompting us, or in what ways we are learning from Jesus. Many of us have begun to feel awkward about thanking God for things of meaning in our everyday lives, or pointing to God's goodness.

When we walk with Jesus, and have an openness to talk about him, such conversations become more comfortable. Whenever we do something we love, or have a wonderful experience, it is natural to share about it. This is the same with our relationship with Jesus. There is a greater ease to putting words to your faith after you . . . well, start putting words to your faith. Imagine if you talked about sex throughout your day, at various points. If you're the easily embarrassed type, that flush of red that hits your cheeks would diminish over time. In the same way, as we talk about Jesus, our spiritual walk, our experience of the Spirit in our lives, and our experience of God in our day-to-day lives, we will grow in our ability to articulate that to our kids.

Because when you really care about something, you find a way to explain it clearly to your children. And when you care about it deeply, it comes up over and over and over again.

WHAT GOES WITHOUT SAYING SOON GOES WITHOUT DOING

When my husband was a teenager, his mom used to shout all kinds of things to him as he left the house for school or an activity. At first, her reminders were a simple few things: Drive safely! Be wise. Honor Jesus. And so forth.

As time went on, however, Becky Frisk's list became longer. While this next part is now a point of some contention in the Frisk family, my husband says that her list became so obviously prescriptive that he would roll his eyes whenever she chimed off her list of safety dos and don'ts and Christlike reminders. The list mounted over time so that my husband eventually said to his mother, "Geez, Mom, why don't you just tell me to remember to breathe?"

And so she did—and has continued to do so for many years. In fact, "Don't forget to breathe!" has become an important reminder to my husband many times as he has parted ways with his mother. And while it will always remain a joke for us, "Don't forget to breathe!" is simply one of many obvious statements we make that land in the "it goes without saying" category.

Our families all have oodles of things that land in that category. Brush your teeth before leaving the house. Ask before using something that belongs to someone else. Don't be a jerk. In fact, our churches have many things that "go without saying" too. And while the things that go without saying are, at first, painstakingly obvious—Don't forget to breathe!—over time, they become less and less so. What happens is this: Things go without saying, so no one says them. Soon no one remembers how to do them or even what they are. What goes without saying becomes things that we end up going without entirely.

But I think that the things that have gone without saying for too long need to be said again. When it comes to discipling our own kids, many of the things that used to go without saying have stopped being said altogether. Eventually, over time, when things stop being said, those things stop happening, because no one is familiar with them anymore.

For example, it used to go without saying that Christians pray before meals, and teach their kids how to navigate the Bible, and give generously to the church and other compassionate organizations. But these things have gone without saying for too long. When we stop talking with our kids about what it looks like, practically, to follow Jesus, that idea will recede into the background. Eventually they won't have any idea what any of this stuff even means.

FROM ROTE EXERCISE TO JOYFUL PRACTICE

Practices like these—praying, reading Scripture, giving—fall by the wayside, first in our conversations and then in our lives, for many reasons. Once when I was teaching a Jesus-centered parenting course to a group of parents, I asked them what spiritual practices, if any, existed in their families of origin. One woman spoke of a daily dinner time that included prayer and Bible reading. When she said this, I thought, how lovely! But then she told the group that this practice was deeply frustrating for her as a child, because it was more of a rote exercise than much else. She knew her parents placed a very high value on reading the Bible and praying together, but she was frustrated by the feeling that all of this came without discussion of application or space for questions or conversation about what had just been read.

As she wrestled through this, she realized that now, as a parent, she wanted to do these practices with her own family but that she would make the adjustments she wished were present when she was a child. For her family of origin, it had gone without saying that prayer and Bible reading were important. But what needed to be said—and wasn't—was that asking questions about and discussing Scripture was also encouraged. She needed the *why* behind the *what*, and she now had the opportunity to provide both to her own children.

THE PRACTICE OF PRAYER

When it comes to praying before meals, some families do this as a sort of family tradition or ritual. Others pick it up once they have children because their kids learn it at a Christian daycare or school. Others stumble back into it for a special occasion or holiday. Some traditions and rituals are helpful, and consistency matters; still, a ritual without meaning is pointless.

Prayer before meals can be an amazing example to our children of gratitude, of thanksgiving, of our need for God and God's great care for us. But words devoid of attention and awareness to what we are doing are meaningless. In our house, every once in a while, we have to remind ourselves why we pray before a meal. My husband will ask our daughter, "Why do we pray at dinner?" And she usually considers the question for a moment and then responds, "To thank God for our food." We get to talk to God any time of day, but pausing at specific moments throughout our day to reflect and thank God is an act of goodness. It doesn't only have to be at mealtimes, but mealtimes can be a great prompt to pause.

Another prayer prompt for me occurs when I am driving and an ambulance passes by with lights flashing and sirens blaring. I usually pray for the person, or people, who are waiting for help. I've done this for years without telling anyone. Then one day, when my daughter was about three years old, an ambulance raced by and she asked me where it was going. We talked about how the ambulance goes to where someone is sick or hurt in order to help them. I looked at her in the rearview mirror and saw that her little three-year-old brow was furrowed. "Do you want to pray for them?" I asked. She said yes.

Thus began something more than just a new prayer time for the two of us. This incident made me realize that there were things in my mind and heart and in my walk with Jesus that I know and do "on the inside"—things that I had not yet shared with my child. If I never talk about this kind of prayer practice with her, she won't know anything about it. So how would I expect her to learn to do it herself?

THE PRACTICE OF READING SCRIPTURE

I mentioned earlier that my mom read her Bible each morning before we got out of bed, but we always saw her just as she was finishing up. I'm not sure if this was intentional, or just the way things worked out. But as kids, my brothers and I saw our mom every morning with her Bible in one hand and her coffee in the other, thus teaching us two valuable lessons in one. Without fail, she would also read the Bible to us each night before we went to bed. I like to think that she bookended each day with the Bible. This practice became embedded within me so much that, when I became old enough to read, I began to read the Bible on my own.

And to encourage our Bible reading, my mom would find devotional books and pick up *Our Daily Bread* for us to read as we grew older. My mother was also involved in what we learned in Sunday school and at vacation Bible school (if you didn't grow up going to church, think summer Christian day camp), and she ensured that we knew how to find our books of the Bible, chapter and verse. While she never explicitly said, "I am now going to teach you how to look things up in the Bible," she did just that, and she did it well (please don't tell her, or she might get a big head!).

As a curriculum pastor for kids and youth, I now ensure that I write ideas into lesson plans on how to best navigate Bibles and how to encourage regular Scripture reading so that children who come to church on their own and children whose parents are helping them encounter Jesus know how to look up passages in their Bibles and know what to read. It may go without saying that we who love Scripture will teach our kids how to navigate their Bibles and find certain stories and passages, and that we will share with them why we care about Scripture. But these are things we should start saying—and doing—again.

THE PRACTICE OF WORSHIP

Something else that has been surprisingly interesting to verbalize with our daughter is how and why we worship God. When you think about it, worship can be a tough concept to communicate. The most obvious experience of this is musical worship. Musical worship is more than just singing some songs together; you can do that at karaoke night at any local pub. Musical worship has something intangible to it. We are directing our hearts to God. We are focusing on and connecting with God in an experiential way. Whether it is in a communal setting during a church service or while singing solo in the car, kitchen, or shower, when we focus on God in this way, it realigns our hearts and reminds us of how good our God is. The inevitable reaction is worship.

When I asked my daughter once why we worship God, she said, "Because he is *our* God." That's what we do. We worship God. Because God is our God and he is good, and he loves us. That's the least we can do. As we stand and sing in our church service, I stand beside my daughter and try to explain anything in the lyrics that may be confusing or complicated. I am aware that I am her guide through all of this. If my husband or I don't tell her, who will?

Our kids may enjoy the music that we hear in our church on a Sunday, or they might not. Even if our kids don't want to engage in the musical worship at our church, it doesn't mean they don't enjoy any musical worship. A beautiful part of the kingdom of God is that there are so many different ways to sing our praise to God. And if musical worship isn't your child's thing at all, that's okay too. Musical worship may not be a way that your child can really connect well. Children may find certain music, or pitches, or people distracting. Opening our kids up to a variety of worship options is an awesome opportunity we have as parents. We'll talk more about what these are in an upcoming chapter.

THE PRACTICE OF GIVING

In my family when I was growing up, we didn't talk very much about money. That's probably because we didn't really have any. And so, for me, the awkward talking point—perhaps as sex or Jesus is for other families—used to be money. But I'm talking my way out of that awkwardness. So let's talk money for a minute, shall we?

It used to go without saying that Christians gave to the church. The church only stays afloat by the giving of its people. There is no secret fund, no government subsidy, no holy cash cow. While you may know that, there has been a bit of silence in church culture—at least in my experience—about what or why we give to the church. As a child and teen in the

Pentecostal church, I remember passionate "offering calls," the lead-up to giving the offering, that were as long as the sermon. More often than not, they felt like massive biblical guilt trips.

But that's not the point. The early church shared all they had together. They cared for one another and for the poor (Acts 2:44-45). If the church in one region found out that another church community in another region was in need, that church provided. The concept was that all money really was God's money. A friend of mine has taken to referring to money as "kingdom dollars." My money isn't mine; it's God's. So I need to connect with God's desire for those funds. Obviously, some of those funds need to go to the life essentials, such as housing and groceries. But most of us have other funds about which we need to ask, "God, what do you want for this money?"

It could be easy to pay off all the things that we deem "essential" and then give God the leftovers. But as we place our trust in God, we actually begin to give to God first. It's completely counterintuitive and upside down, but such is the kingdom of God. As we steward these kingdom dollars, we are doing so out of a glad heart. In 2 Corinthians 9:7-8, Paul writes to the church in Corinth, "You must each decide in your heart how much to give. And don't give reluctantly or in response to pressure. 'For God loves a person who gives cheerfully.' And God will generously provide all you need. Then you will always have everything you need and plenty left over to share with others." I need this reminder often, and it's one for us to teach our kids. Imagine what our world would look like if all disciples everywhere were actually doing this! What a beautiful world it would be.

Once again, as we do these things, it is helpful to talk about giving, so that our kids know that is a thing we do, out of our love for Jesus. (You may not want to share an actual amount, unless you don't mind everyone knowing your financial choices—turns out that kids have no filter and may share that kind of thing freely.) The previous generations' mind-set was that the right hand shouldn't know what the left was doing (Matthew 6:3). And it's true: we shouldn't flaunt or boast about our giving. Yet when it comes to discipling our own kids, we can help them learn stewardship by letting them in on how we give to the church and helping them consider this whole idea of stewarding kingdom dollars.

Since the time our daughter was about two years old, she has had three jars on a shelf in our living room. They are labeled Live, Save, and Give. When she earns money or receives it for birthdays or Christmas, she chooses how much of each goes into what jar. (There is sometimes a little parental guidance, but usually very little is needed.) The Live jar is for fun, everyday sorts of things: a pack of gum, a lollipop. The Save jar is for things that she wants to save up for. Her current goal is to save for a telescope. And then there's the Give jar, which holds money that she will give to the church or a nonprofit organization that helps others.

When my daughter was about two and a half, we used to send her to her Sunday school class with a couple of quarters, maybe a dollar, that we would scoop out of her Give jar. As she grew older, we began to ask her to go and get money from her jar herself. One day, she came back with a couple of dollars, and she asked, "Is this enough?" I said, "Well, it's up to you. What would you like to take?" She asked, "What does the money do?" I told her that it went to help other people hear about Jesus. Her eyes went wide, and she went back to retrieve another dollar. My heart swelled. This was one of those parenting win moments you write in your diary for the challenging days and nights ahead. The truth is that being generous with our money gets more difficult when we forget *why* we give. Reminding our kids of the *why* behind the *what* will form their stewardship experience for life.

This isn't limited to our monetary giving either. Explaining to our children (and reminding our teens!) *why* we serve in various settings is beneficial. It is not about collecting community service hours for a college application, or because it makes us feel good; rather, we serve in our church and in our community because we are the hands and feet of Jesus in the world. He sends us to continue to do the amazing work of building the kingdom. Sometimes that simply means showing up somewhere, and other times it means getting our hands (literally) dirty. The practice of giving is to reexamine and realize that we have an abundance given to us by God and that we can give from that abundance.

SAY THE *WHY* BEHIND THE *WHAT*

While it could be crystal clear in your family that it goes without saying that y'all love Jesus, Jesus is Lord, the church is an important part of life, you are on mission with Jesus, you care for others, and so on: still, I really do believe it needs to be said. And said often. Again, when things that "go without saying" go without being said for long enough, people forget how to say them. We forget to actually articulate the things we take for granted. When that continues for long enough, people forget those things altogether.

One of the things that may be most helpful to do in your own spiritual journey—and your journey as a Jesus-centered parent—is to consider the things that "go without saying" in your own family. Does it go without saying that you always pray before a meal? Make it known. Actually say what you do and *why* you do it. Does it go without saying that you give financially to your church or make donations to other organizations? Say it and do it. Let your kids know that you give and why you do. Does it go without saying that you value people over things? Let your kids know that, and model it. Does it go without saying that your church community is a vital part of your life? Let your kids know that, and help them believe it by being present and involved. Does it go without saying that helping others is important? That reading the Bible is a value? That prayer matters? Say these things out loud. Say them again. And be sure to make your words mean something by doing those things.

It may seem exhausting to be a commentator of your own spiritual life. Don't get me wrong: I'm not asking you to share with your child every single tidbit of your quiet time with Jesus (it may be a little less quiet that way). But I do want to encourage you to spend some of it that way. Showing and telling our kids about our own walks with Jesus will help them develop theirs.

It may feel as if you are being a broken record, but go ahead. Be a broken record by the way you love your kids. Be a broken record by the way you love others. Be a broken record by the way you love Jesus. And don't let it all go without saying.

~~DON'T~~ TRY THIS AT HOME

- What are the things from your own upbringing that you recall as the things that went without saying?
- Are there things in your home today that "go without saying" that are worth talking about in your family?

7

SAY AND DO

Children have never been very good at listening to their elders,
but they have never failed to imitate them.
—James Baldwin

I've never been great at reading the rules for games. I get lost in the instructions, because they mean very little when I don't see them played out before me. I'd rather have someone show me a game and explain it while we go. The explanation is helpful when it helps all the actions connect. And if I happen to miss a rule, I'd rather learn it on the fly than have to catalog it in a list of instructions that are read aloud. Show me while you tell me, or I really won't understand.

This tells me that I learn better by seeing an example or doing something with someone than by being told what to do. The great majority of people learn this way. We may need explanations as we go, but we also need to be *shown*.

In the previous chapter we looked at what we can say to our children about following Jesus. As we saw, the saying—the explaining of what we are doing and why—is important. But actually following through on what we say is also crucial. In this chapter we're going to explore what we, as parents who are raising disciples, can say and what we can *do*. In chapters 8 through 14, then, we will further flesh out what Jesus-centered parenting looks like during specific times, ages, and stages of our children's lives.

As we launch into this section, there are some very real answers we must consider together first. What we show and tell our children about Jesus comes from our own experience and knowledge of what it means to follow Jesus. If that's the case, let's take a look at these questions:

- What does it really look like to follow Jesus in our everyday lives?
- When we say, "Jesus is Lord," what does that really mean to us?
- How do we show and tell our kids what an active faith in Jesus looks like?

Let's look to Jesus to start to answer these questions. First, Jesus lived a life that followed Jewish commandments, and while his relationship with the commandments was slightly complicated, he taught us the most important of the commandments in Matthew 22. The story goes like this: There were experts in the religious law, the spiritual elite of the day, and they were trying to trap Jesus with their very best questions. (I wonder how often I still try to trap Jesus with my questions. But I digress.) One of them asked, "Teacher, what is the most important commandment in the law of Moses?" (Matthew 22:36).

Without missing a beat, and to their great dismay, Jesus responded, "'You must love the Lord your God with all your heart, all your soul, and all your mind.' This is the first and greatest commandment. A second is equally important: 'Love your neighbor as yourself'" (vv. 37-38).

In other words, love God with your whole self, from the inside out and everywhere in between, and love your neighbor in the same way that you love yourself. Let the love of God that you experience spill out everywhere and love others with it. These are the most important directions. Jesus points at and enfleshes these two commandments in his everyday life. So as we begin to consider how to follow Jesus, this is a great start: loving God and loving others.

In the Gospels' accounts of his life and ministry, Jesus again communicates what it takes to follow him. Speaking to an interested crowd, he says, "If any of you wants to be my follower, you must give up your own way, take up your cross daily, and follow me" (Luke 9:23). Every parent I have ever known feels that they are taking up their cross daily, as we die to ourselves for the sake of our kids. But as we die to ourselves, it isn't meant to be for the sake of our kids but for the sake of Christ. Reevaluating our own version of this "dying to self," and reorienting around Christ, will help us in how we show and tell. And I must say, some of us are better at showing than telling. Some are better at telling than showing. This is our opportunity to learn from the side of that coin that isn't our natural tendency.

So as we consider what to say and what to do in discipling our children, we need to consider what we believe are essentials of following Jesus. It's one thing to say "I follow Jesus"; it's another to live out what that means.

SURRENDER

Taking up our cross looks like surrendering to the way of Jesus and committing to look to him as we follow him. Surrender is a daily choice. It means we are letting go of our own way and asking for God to guide our way instead. Surrender takes on a listening stance. Once we surrender our own way of doing, we must be willing to commit to God's way of doing, and in the gaps and places where we aren't sure, we need to be willing to listen. (Which honestly takes patience, and that's a practice all its own. And friend, it is hard!) We listen to God through Scripture, we listen to God through prayer, and we listen to God through the voices in our spiritual community.

Each of these three "listening" exercises can be done in a variety of ways, and we tend to categorize these things into what we call spiritual practices. Spiritual practices include, but certainly aren't limited to, community acts of celebration, time together, hospitality, worship, meditation, centering prayer, imaginative prayer, *lectio divina* ("divine reading"), liturgical prayer, solitude, silence, and fasting. Each of these practices draws us into closer community with the Father, Son, and Spirit. Each of these practices makes us more attentive listeners to what God wants to say to us and, in turn, helps direct us in our lives. Additionally, being consistent in spiritual practices in our own lives allows our kids to see what it is like for their parents to listen to God's voice. While we do this, we are modeling something incredibly important.

We need not feel as though we must be rule-based in our practices; rather, we can aim to be humbly consistent. And all of this—as we listen and orient our lives toward Jesus, actively loving God and loving our neighbors in what we say, disregarded her instructions. Which was often. But I don't think I knew how that Ephesians passage continued until I was well into young adulthood: "Children, obey your parents because you belong to the Lord, for this is the right thing to do. 'Honor your father and mother.' This is the first commandment with a promise: If you honor your father and mother, 'things will go well for you, and you will have a long life on the earth.' [Parents], do not provoke your children to anger by the way you treat them. Rather, bring them up with the discipline and instruction that comes from the Lord" (Ephesians 6:1-4).

Parents, did you hear that? I read that with genuine awareness for the first time in my late teens, and I really wanted to go back to my childhood self so that I could be armed with that text to quote right back to my parents. I wanted to fight back. As a parent now, I know that our kids know how to push our buttons, but if we were really honest with ourselves, we would acknowledge that we know how to push theirs. So when we read, "Parents, do not provoke your children to anger by the way you treat them," it is something that is worth reminding ourselves of every so often. It's a Scripture that is worth sitting with for a while. It's worth a reflection.

Unfortunately, church services and parenting courses don't give this idea—of not provoking our kids to anger—a lot of airtime. But our actions really, truly matter. When we say we love our kids, *showing* them that we do is really important too. Not provoking them is one way. What this looks like in practical terms for toddlers is not escalating the explosive behaviors of a tantrum by yelling at them, but instead speaking soothingly to them and being willing to hold them close. What this looks like for middle schoolers is not yelling and getting in their face when they develop an attitude, but

instead asking the question behind the emotion and reminding them of who they really are.

It's true: as parents, we can be annoying to our kids. We
can get frustrated when our kids perceive us that way, but
we need to admit that we can be obnoxious. (The obnoxious
parent in me wants to hashtag the phrase #sorrynotsorry, but
I'll hold myself back.) Protecting kids of a certain age from
detrimental influences may seem obnoxious to them, but that
is simply the work of parenthood and can't be classified as
provoking them to anger. There is a fine line between being
obnoxious because of the genuine love we show and being
obnoxious because we are actively provoking our kids to
anger. Throughout our children's entire lives, we have the
responsibility to maintain our awareness of that line. As
obnoxious as we might be, we want our kids to know we
are always doing what we do out of love. We need to show
and tell them that in every age and stage. We need to tell
them we love them and to stop in times of stress or joy and
remind them we love them. We need to be consistent with
how we love them. Consistency throughout their lifetime is
so important.

"I love you even when things aren't good."

"I love you even when you do something I don't like."

"I love you even when you do something that others say
is 'bad.'"

"I love you always. Always. Always."

LEARNING TO LAMENT

The more we can model this type of love, the more we are
modeling the love of God the Father. How do we model
God's love throughout their lives? We exhibit it with our own

spiritual lives, and we model it with open and honest communication. That might look like sharing with our kids what we are doing when we are immersed in spiritual practices (prayer, reading the Bible, questions or wonderings about God, serving). Or it might mean sharing our faith journey honestly, at an age-appropriate level, with our kids.

Let me give you a real-time example from my life. We gather with our home church community once a week. Think small group on steroids: families, singles, young and old together one night a week to digest Sunday's content and make it applicable to our lives, and to pray for one another, encourage each other, and eat together. The adults in our home church have been discussing lament. Lately there have been many things to lament: health problems, marriage breakdowns, societal issues—the list could go on and on. And while we have been doing that as adults, we have been grappling with how to engage in this topic with our kids in an appropriate way. While driving in my car later in the week after having this conversation in my home church, my daughter and I stumbled into a conversation on the topic. It began something like this:

> Me: Erin, did you know that you can pray to God about anything?
>
> Erin: Well, yeah.
>
> Me: Did you know you can even tell God that you are frustrated or having a tough day?
>
> Erin: Oh? I didn't really know.
>
> Me: You can. Anytime. Even when things are hard, you can talk to God about it.

Check. I gave her an additional tip on connecting with God. Good for me. She received a glimpse of the idea of lament, and by not probing her on what hard or frustrating things she might be facing, I saved her from having to face hard things in that moment of time. I thought it was a passing Mom-talks-Erin-listens moment. We need those moments as parents.

And then *another* school shooting happened.

Erin doesn't miss a thing. Her ears are wide open. I happened to be listening to the news on the radio when the school shooting was mentioned. Seventeen deaths. Shot by a former student. The level of tragedy was unreal.

Erin's head popped up. The conversation began again, in a different way.

Erin: Mom, did they say a student shot kids at school?

Me: Yeah, kiddo, they did. It's sad, isn't it?

Erin: But, Mom, why? Why would that happen? God, why would that happen?

Me: That is a good question to ask. And we don't know. But we do know that the shooter was a very sad boy who needed help.

Erin: So he wasn't just a bad guy?

Me: No, he wasn't just a bad guy. He was a very sad boy who didn't really have a family.

Erin: Oh, that's so sad.

It is sad, my baby. It is sad.

Later that night, when we were reflecting on and praying about the day. I told Erin this was a time when it makes a lot of sense to use that new kind of prayer we had talked about in home church: lament. She prayed, "Why, God? Why did this happen? We don't understand. We just want to know why. It's so sad. So many kids dead. But why, God?" I held her, and I did our regular nighttime liturgy, and I cried a little while I sang "I'll Love You Forever" and rocked her back and forth, back and forth, back and forth.

Lament is not an easy spiritual practice to learn, but it is immensely important. Our kids need to know that even as they walk in the way of Jesus, they can turn to God when things are difficult and simply ask why. They need to know that they can wrestle with God and grieve and call out to God in sadness or frustration or pain. Unfortunately, this practice has been largely omitted from the Western church for decades now. We fear emotional outrage and reaction to pain, so we sanitize things a little so that we don't have to deal with the collective pain. But half the psalms are laments to God. There is a great deal of biblical precedent for calling out to God in pain and disillusionment. Sitting with pain and grief, and joining with Jesus in lament: we need to be able to model this to our kids so that they know that they do not need to hide their grief from God. They can take it to God directly, and they can face the pain of the world with Jesus at their side.

That's one example of what saying and doing looks like in our home at the moment. The saying and doing of faith may look very different for you and your family at this time and place in your lives. If you have a two-year-old, the most basic form of lament might be saying that we can tell Jesus when we are sad. A more advanced form of this, for a teenager, might be encouraging your teen to write out a prayer of lament or driving them far out in the countryside and shout out their pain to God.

Every step of the journey looks different in every home, but the underlying principle is the same: say and do. As you discover a spiritual practice and wade into its waters, share about that experience with your children. For example, if you discover the beauty of sitting with Jesus in a contemplative way, share about what you've experienced around the dinner table. If you're able, invite your children to experience some of it for themselves. Always invite; never demand.

For example, you could invite your middle schooler or teen into that practice with you. Light a candle and be still while you focus on Jesus. It doesn't have to be an exorbitant amount of time; let your child set the time they feel comfortable with. Or perhaps you've been being more mindful to practice forgiveness, and you've journeyed into some difficult relationships in which you needed to find a way to forgive. Share that experience with your child. Invite them to consider the same thoughts. Invite them to consider the questions: Is there anyone that you are holding a grudge against? What do you think it would take to forgive that person?

A shared spiritual practice can be an extraordinary thing, but I repeat: always invite; never demand. A spiritual practice that is forced will leave a horrible taste in the mouth. A spiritual practice that is offered freely will create a positive imprint in a young person's memory and life.

~~DON'T~~ TRY THIS AT HOME

- What are you *doing*? That is, what ways are you living out your faith? Are you engaged in your own spiritual practices that you can talk about with your children? If not, consider looking into what spiritual practices you can explore over the coming weeks.
- What are you *saying*? Are you having a hard time finding the words to share with your child? If so, find another adult who is great at breaking things down and

8

STAGES OF SPIRITUAL DEVELOPMENT

Becoming like Christ is a long, slow process of growth.
—Rick Warren

When our children are born, we worry about them hitting all their developmental markers. Is she rolling over when she should? Is he learning the right sounds? Is she being socialized enough? Are his teeth coming in when they are supposed to? Why isn't he interested in potty training yet? How long until she will sleep through the night?

It is fair to say that at some point every parent in the history of the world has worried about something. (Except maybe Mary and Joseph . . . then again, maybe they worried more than the rest of us. I mean, raising the Lord and Savior of the entire world may involve a little parental pressure.) Caring for a vulnerable human being and shaping someone into a full-fledged larger human really is a major responsibility. It's equal parts humbling, exciting, and terrifying.

Thankfully, birth parents get nine months, give or take, to prepare for that little bean to enter the world. Foster and adoptive parents have some space between fostering classes or the many forms to be filled out and evaluations to be completed before adoption. We plan for our children in so many ways. For babies we prepare to birth: we make a birth plan, we get their little onesies and sleepers washed and ready, we decide on diapers, we prepare their sleeping scenario, we go to midwife or doctor appointments, we take vitamins, we make a list of names, and on and on. For fostering or adoption, there are home studies, picking out the right sheet sets, and making sure foods align with dietary restrictions. We set and reset our homes to make sure everything is just right.

As we launch into chapters that cover various ages and stages of parenting, may I suggest adding a couple of things to the list—things that I believe are far more important than everything else I just named?

PRAY

Becoming a parent has made me more of a pray-er than any other experience in my life. Now, with a child, there is this part of me that isn't a part of my physical person. It's as if my heart is walking outside my body in another, smaller body, and I cannot control where she goes or what she does. So I pray and I trust Jesus. Well, more accurately: I pray, and I struggle to trust Jesus. And then I pray some more.

So here's my first task for your to-do list: pray.

1. Pray for that child daily.
2. Pray that your child would know the love of Jesus.

3. Pray that you would be a great example to your child as a disciple and disciple-maker.
4. Pray for your family. Pray, pray, pray.

I realize that "pray about it" sounds like clichéd Christian advice, but I assure you that it is so much more powerful than that. I genuinely believe that God hears us and cares about the prayers of God's people. I believe that God answers our prayers. I believe that God has much more wisdom and knowledge than I do, that God's answers may be very different from the ones I suggest, and that I need to learn to receive that. In prayer, we stare into the great thought of "Let your will be done on earth as it is in heaven." Let our will align with your will. That's big, and that can be difficult, but it can also be beautiful.

I believe that Jesus meant what he said in Matthew 7:

Keep on asking, and you will receive what you ask for. Keep on seeking, and you will find. Keep on knocking, and the door will be opened to you. For everyone who asks, receives. Everyone who seeks, finds. And to everyone who knocks, the door will be opened. You parents—if your children ask for a loaf of bread, do you give them a stone instead? Or if they ask for a fish, do you give them a snake? Of course not! So if you sinful people know how to give good gifts to your children, how much more will your heavenly Father give good gifts to those who ask him. (Matthew 7:7-11)

As we go to God repeatedly on behalf of our kids, as we keep on asking in Jesus' name for things in line with what God desires, the door is opened. And as parents, we just keep praying. And praying. And praying.

Parenting is a surprising and sometimes unsettling experience that stretches my faith and trust. It's hard and beautiful.

So please, take it from me (and my mom, and my mom's mom): Pray. A lot.

Okay, we've started with prayer; let's take the next step. As we equip ourselves physically and emotionally for parenting at every age and stage, we can also become equipped in our own spiritual lives to disciple our kids in the best way we know how.

DISCIPLE AND BE DISCIPLED

I have heard many first-time-expecting parents say that they feel unprepared to be a parent. While we can never truly be prepared, those nine months sure do help in the overall process. Luckily, when it comes to spiritual parenting and preparedness, we are in training for this from day one of being Christ-followers.

How? As Christ-followers, we are disciples. By definition, disciples are disciple-makers. Likewise, spiritual parents are disciple-makers. Literally, you have birthed or adopted a little being whom you now get to disciple. That's exciting! You have an in-house disciple you are raising—a person whom you are helping discover the way of Jesus in a real-life, every-day applicable way.

While we disciple our children, we have the ability to encourage their spiritual development for the first several years of their lives without many external factors coming into play. Our kids are sponges, and they really do absorb all the things that we send their way (regardless of whether we always like it or realize it). Our time as their go-to people lasts for a different range of time for each child, but most studies state that even into the teen years, parents are considered the primary influencer. They watch us, they see what we do, they consider whether we practice what we preach. They take our ideas and try to punch holes in them. They see if these ideas stand fast when storms come their way. They are curious. Our children want to see a level of integrity in what we do and who we say we are, and they will continue to push at those things to see if we hold to them.

As you disciple your mini disciple, you also need to be discipled yourself. Finding parents who are further down the road from you and learning from them is a great start. Spend time with them as they parent—maybe even lend them a hand here and there—and see how they do what they do. Hear how they speak to their kids. Ask questions about and watch how they do spiritual formation with their children. Ask them how and when they pray, read the Bible, and have spiritual conversations with their kids. Ask them how they show their kids that Jesus is the most important part of their lives.

As we are discipled, we become better disciple-makers. The really cool thing about how Jesus taught us to do ministry is to be present with people. And the beautiful thing is that whether we are being discipled or are discipling, we are following Jesus' example of being present with others. That's a gift.

I realize that some introverts who read those last sentences felt an immediate sense of exhaustion. Be not discouraged! Know that there are other introverts who seek to disciple while being aware of the limits they have for time spent with people. Find them. Learn from them. Be discipled by them. Then if you discover that your child is an extrovert, find an extroverted disciple-maker and learn from them. That's the beauty of the kingdom. In communities dedicated to Christ, we have so many people to learn from—people who are wired uniquely and can help us in our unique struggles.

Pray. Disciple and be discipled. These things cover every age and stage of our children's growth. As we learn to pray, we learn what it means to be a disciple. We follow others as they follow Christ. We learn from them, and experience discipleship so that we know how to bring our own children through the process of discipleship.

All this requires us to be constantly on our knees in prayer, from the first moment we learn of our child and through the rest of our lives. Defaulting to Jesus in all things is never a bad thing. If only this were our standard factory setting! Most of us need to train ourselves to do this. Constantly.

And while we do that for ourselves, we can help guide our children in their own spiritual development through the various ages and stages of life. In the next chapters we will look at what it means to disciple children in certain stages; here we will do a brief overview of the ways that psychologists and educators have divided up stages.

AGES AND STAGES

So what are the actual stages that children experience, and how do these relate to discipling? In this section, we'll unpack these ideas a bit and see how these breakdowns can be both helpful and unhelpful. To give you the quickest snapshot of developmental approaches, we will do a drive-through version of the following: Jean Piaget's stages of cognitive development; Erik Erikson's stages of psychosocial development; and James Fowler's stages of faith development. Please know that this is in no way a critique of academic work—that's way above my pay grade. What follows is merely a concise overview of the various concepts at play when we speak about children's spiritual development. While too many descriptors and boxes can muddle our overall understanding, seeing how various thinkers have categorized children's development can be helpful.

Jean Piaget (1896–1980) was, among other things, a developmental psychologist who pioneered work in cognitive development. To this day, educators study his theory as an integral part of their foundational knowledge. Piaget's stages of cognitive development are broken down as follows: sensorimotor (0–2 years), preoperational (2–6 years), concrete operational (7–11 years), and formal operational (12 years–adult). While each stage can be (and has been!) written about in great depth, I will offer an incredibly simple breakdown.

In the first stage, infants and young toddlers rely on their senses and movement to experience, discover, and understand the world. The world that they know and can comprehend is only a world where they are the center. The second stage, preoperational, begins at roughly two years of age, or as a child learns how to talk, and lasts until the end of their sixth year. This stage is characterized in many ways by the imagination. Children in this stage understand and explore the world through imaginative play. They haven't quite arrived at the ability to logically reason, but their capacity for imagination is immense. This is a most beautiful time in their spiritual development, I believe, but we'll get to that.

The third stage, that of the concrete operational function, is a stage in which children aged about seven to eleven cross a threshold into logical thinking and have begun to grow out of their egocentricity. In addition to this, they really only think in their present context without the capacity to think to the future. The final stage of childhood cognitive development is the formal operational stage. Children in this stage are stepping out of childhood and into their adolescent years. From age twelve and beyond, young people begin to develop the ability to think more abstractly and to reason more logically (although that often conflicts with swinging hormones and social conflict, in my humble opinion!).[1]

While these groupings are generally helpful, in some ways they may seem to confine or limit the ability of children's spiritual development within each cognitive stage. But let's pause there for a moment while we turn to developmental psychologist Erik Erikson. Erikson (1902–94) mapped out the stages of psychosocial development from birth to the young adult years, along with the virtue that may be attained during each stage, as follows: basic trust versus basic mistrust, hope (0–18 months); autonomy versus shame and doubt, will (18 months–3 years); initiative versus guilt, purpose (3–5 years); industry versus inferiority, competence (6–11 years); identity versus identity confusion, fidelity (12–18 years); and intimacy versus isolation, love (young adulthood).[2] Erikson's stages do advance further into adulthood; however, for our purposes, we will conclude at this point. For each stage, the child must experience the appropriate levels of nurture and care, as well as opportunity to engage in various experiences in order to develop in the area of the aforementioned virtues. For instance, for infants to develop hope, they must be able to hold in tension the general understanding of basic trust and basic mistrust. Again, this perspective on development can help us understand our child's spiritual development; once again, it can also limit it. These stages of development are based on generalities throughout the ages. The ages are not set in stone but provide a guideline of understanding.

While we consider both Piaget's and Erikson's stages, let us also consider that of James Fowler (1940–2015). In the early 1980s, Fowler, a minister, theologian, and expert in human development, wrote *Stages of Faith*, in which he builds off the work of Piaget and Erikson to establish his own understanding of the stages of faith. The stages are as follows:

- Stage 0 – primal or undifferentiated faith (0–2 years)
- Stage 1 – intuitive-projective faith (3–7 years)
- Stage 2 – mythic-literal faith (7–12 years)
- Stage 3 – synthetic-conventional faith (12+ years)
- Stage 4 – individual-reflective faith (21+ years)
- Stage 5 – conjunctive faith (35+ years)
- Stage 6 – universalizing faith (later adult years, if at all)

To get a glimpse of what each of these means, let's consider a few simple explanations. Young children in stage 0, or the primal stage, understand God on the basis of their physical and emotional surroundings. A child who has a positive, secure, and safe upbringing will likely have a positive understanding of God. Fowler states that "the seeds of trust, courage, hope and love are fused in an undifferentiated way and contend with sensed threats of abandonment, inconsistencies, and deprivations in an infant's environment."[3] If someone had a tumultuous childhood or experience of neglect during this time, that person's view of God will be more negative.

Stage 1 occurs when much of the faith journey is discovered through narrative, absorbed through experience, and observed in important people. Images and symbols are significant to children during this time, as is the power of their own imaginations. Stage 2 brings with it the need for clear, logical, and literal stories. These stories are worn like a sports jersey to show that the child belongs to that team. In stage 3, adolescents face the external pressures of peers and culture in a way that begins to shape their identity and faith. Adolescents synthesize their faith according to what they are experiencing in the world around them, what they value, and how they are shaped by their caregivers' faith. However, this is still a rather unexamined faith overall.

Stage 4 arises as young adults face a crisis of faith or identity in which the foundations of their childhood faith are shaken. This may happen as the result of having too many holes poked in what have been their faith foundations, or simply the experience of leaving home and trying to discern who they are.[4]

Stage 4 is, in more modern expression, a dive into deconstruction. Young adults at this stage are taking a true look at their belief systems, potentially for the very first time, and may choose to drop them and walk away or to take on their own belief sets. This is a very accurate depiction of what we often see in the lives of older teens and young adults who leave home for school, work, or exploration.[5] Some may remain in this stage of faith development longer than others, as this is a stage in which one must be willing to grapple with the messy realities of faith, beliefs, practice, and the many inconsistencies that there may be between them all.

Fowler suggests that the next stage doesn't generally begin until the mid- to late thirties. He says stage 5 is a complex stage to describe and define. It is a stage in which the adult is willing to hold in comfortable tension the many contradictions, inconsistencies, and paradoxes that exist while holding firmly to the core truth of the faith. In this stage, the adult would be able to interact with people of various faith traditions while not feeling conflict with their own. The final stage, which I will only briefly mention here, is one that, according to Fowler, few adults reach. Stage 6 is a universalizing faith in which the adult is completely decentered and the focus of the faith is on attributes such as love, justice, and peace.

Whether it is Fowler's stages, or Erikson's, or Piaget's, each can be helpful to understand the collective or generic development of children (or adolescents or adults); however, when we get to the individual child, these categories may be tossed out the window. These stages act as a way to generally categorize the individual, not as a blueprint. Some parents see a similar range in expectations in their children's cognitive development as well as notice their little ones developing ahead of their peers. Other parents may notice a heightened emotional intelligence in their children. Kids, who one minute are playing a silly game and the next minute are expressing spiritual insight far beyond their years, are difficult to so clearly catalog. Some may struggle in school or in social relationships or with their emotions, but they may also unmistakably grasp and understand the spiritual.

This leaves us space in our categorical charts for something that we, too, can't quite pin down: the Holy Spirit. When the Holy Spirit is active in a child, we cannot possibly think we can categorize the work of the Spirit in a simple way. As one friend of mine said to me, "There is no junior Holy Spirit." When the Spirit joins with our spirit, we cannot possibly ascertain the development work that God is doing. Each child is unique in this way.

With all these theories, stages, thoughts, and ideas out in the open, let's piece together some concrete ideas, by age, to guide us into fruitful (and fun!) discipleship of our children.

~~DON'T~~ TRY THIS AT HOME

- In what way has parenting altered your prayer life? What is the role of prayer in your daily life?
- Do you have someone who is discipling you? If not, is there someone you would consider asking? Or perhaps this is something to start praying about?
- What are the spiritual practices that you have, or would like to have, with your child or children?

9

RED BALL: BIRTH TO AGE TWO

A person's a person, no matter how small.
– Dr. Seuss

Congratulations, you are now responsible for a living, breathing human! The adoption is complete, or the baby made its way into the world. That reality didn't fully hit me until my husband and I were leaving the hospital with our infant daughter a couple of days postbirth. As we put our daughter into her car seat, the thought that ran through my mind was, "Who is letting us do this?" My husband and I weren't all that young—we were both in our later twenties—and I still felt we must be way too young to be parents, way too inexperienced to be responsible for the life of a fragile human being.

So I did what every new mother who feels way out of her depth does: I read blog posts, websites, articles, and books. I asked questions. I talked to other parents. While there are many amazing resources on what to expect in the first year or so of life and how to best support your child's physical/mental/emotional/social development—honestly, the market on all these areas is saturated with content!—fewer resources exist that focus on a child's spiritual development. In fact, many well-meaning people look at infants and think, "They're babies. What could they possibly learn about Jesus at this stage?" Bless them, I understand the thinking, but are they ever wrong.

Consider this: You are holding a small baby in your arms. You may be singing to them or talking silly to them (why do we do that?), or pointing out items around the room trying to help them match words with objects. You might say, "See this *red ball*?" while showing the baby a red ball because we want kids to know their colors, and their shapes, and simple objects very early on. We are always teaching infants and toddlers, because they are *always* learning. Children from birth to eighteen months are experiencing one of the fastest rates of growth that they will have in their entire lives. They are little sponges, soaking up every tidbit of information. Are they able to regurgitate all that information back to you? No, of course not. But they are learning the most foundational things that will continue to develop as they develop. If we didn't help babies with their colors, numbers, sounds, shapes, and simple objects, we'd worry that their development would be stunted. They're just babies; what can they learn? The answer is the foundation to an eternal faith in Jesus.

What then do we do, practically speaking, with our children at this age? We narrate. We tell our little ones what we are doing. We share our lives with them. We pray aloud. We bounce them on our laps as we read the Bible. We clean up their puke and try to cling to the promise of the Spirit's work in our lives. We tell them that Jesus loves them. We sing aloud: hymns, songs, and spiritual songs. We get excited about going to church gatherings, and we help them get excited too. We put their inaugural attempt at coloring in their Sunday school class on the fridge. We pray some more. As they start to show some interest in books, we read them children's Bible stories, again, and again, and again—because repetition is so important, and you can't get enough of a good thing. I'll say it again: repetition is so important!

Our little wonders are picking up so much from us. They are experiencing connection with us and learning what it means to be loved by us. They discover sounds, smells, tastes, and touches and then find their voice—oh, I love when they find their voice and start to gurgle and coo their early praises to Jesus. They are also recognizing how they feel. They know that certain sounds make them feel happy or calm, and others make them scared or sad.

As we talk to them, and sing, and narrate our way through their lives, they come to feel secure in our voices and in our tunes (no matter how tone deaf we may be, and I speak from experience here). Soon our growing babies-almost-toddlers begin to discover the enjoyment of stories. This is when a good children's Bible is absolutely priceless. When you read your child a Bible story—may I recommend centering on stories of Jesus from the Gospels as much as possible in their formative toddler years—they will, at some point, inevitably shout their request to you, "Again! Again!" That is just the best. When a young child requests more Bible stories, read more. You might not feel up to it after the eleventh time, but do it anyway. Help that little person know that story inside and out.

Next, I want to encourage you to take that little bean to church. I know what some of you are thinking: "They'll never know if they went to church at this age; they'll never remember. Besides, mornings are hard with a little one. We'll start going to church when they are just a little older." Trust me, no judgment here! I do understand this impulse. It is tiring to just have a baby, and trying to get out of the house, especially in the morning, is a huge challenge. And once you get to church, who knows if that baby will stay in the nursery, or if they do, they may become a smoking volcano ready to erupt at any moment. While all this may be true, I'd strongly encourage you to gather with a local body of Christ in these early years. Children—and babies in particular—are such a gift to the church community, and in return, the church community can be such a gift to our small children and to our families. When kids learn to know trusted adults who care about them and with whom they feel safe, the body of Christ becomes a true gift to us as parents and to our children. We genuinely need one another. The church *community* is meant to be church *family*. This extended family can be extra hands in a difficult time and extra spiritual parents throughout our kids' lives: it can mean extra huggers, extra candy-givers, extra loving people showing our kids the kingdom of God. This is important stuff, my friends, and I genuinely believe that helping even our youngest children feel a sense of belonging in a church is an essential part of discipling the next generation.

These wise early choices—to narrate to our little ones, pray with and for them, take them to church, and so forth—shape our children's upbringing, as do other spiritual experiences that we can pray for but not necessarily plan for. This chapter would be incomplete if I didn't say what I am about to say next. I will warn you in advance that it may sound a little strange, and also that I have no real theological foundation for what I'm about to say. But this claim is based both on what I have witnessed—anecdotal evidence—and on a genuine belief that when Jesus said the kingdom of heaven belongs to those who become like little children, he was telling the truth.

Here it goes: I think that small children are spiritually attuned in a way that we as adults cannot quite comprehend. I think that they have an extra special link to the spiritual world. A memory from my daughter's early years is burned into my mind. She was pre-verbal but was walking and learning so much. She had just begun to really master giving high fives when we had some friends over to our house. They were just about to leave when I said to my daughter, "Give everyone a high five." And she did. She made her way around the room, giving high fives to each person—and then in a space where no one was standing (no one we could see, anyway), she gave another high five in the air. I'm not saying that there was an angelic being in the room, but I'm not discounting it either.

There's another story, from my niece's young life, that floats in my mind. It gives me chills every time I tell it. My niece went running to her parents' bedroom in the morning. She said, "Mom! Dad! I just had a dream that I was in heaven with God and he said, 'I love you and I love your mom and dad. Now wake up and go and tell them.' And so I did."

My brother and sister-in-law were stunned. What a way to wake up! After a moment, my sister-in-law asked her, "What did God look like?" My niece replied, "He was so colorful, Mom. He was so many different colors." (Revelation 4:3 says, "The glow of an emerald circled his throne like a rainbow.")

Again, I've got no helpful studies to cite here, and I am not a psychological or educational expert. But as a pastor, I do know some things about spirituality, and I must say that babies, toddlers, and small children have a heightened spiritual connection that we just can't quantify. This is what I know to be true: the kingdom of heaven belongs to the childlike. As parents and teachers and pastors, we do not necessarily need to theologically fine-tune or correct the spiritual sensibility of a young child at this age; we simply need to encourage it.

Here, then, are some concrete suggestions for you to consider as you nourish these sweet children of the Most High God.

~~DON'T~~ TRY THIS AT HOME

- *Pray with your little one.* Pray prayers of thanks, prayers of help, and prayers of hope. Pray the Lord's Prayer. Pray one-sentence prayers. Bookend your day in prayer. Pray thanks to God out loud for a new day with your little one. Pray as a part of a bedtime routine. Pray without ceasing. Pray in your quiet thoughts, and pray aloud so that your children experience your talks with God too. Make it simple and clear. "Dear God, thank you for . . ."; "Dear God, please help . . ."; "Dear God, you are . . ." ; "Dear God, I need . . ." Oh, and while you are praying with and for your child, invite a couple of friends or mentors to commit to praying for your child as your child grows. When you do this, you are intentionally choosing people whom you want to journey with your child, long term, in prayer. Perhaps someday one or two of them will serve as spiritual mentors for your young person.

- *Sing songs and hymns of worship to Jesus.* Find Jesus-y tunes that your little one will enjoy so that they can experience musical worship at their own level. But play the worship music that you enjoy at times too. Help your child discover the diversity of the music that we sing to show Jesus how much we love him and to better discover how much he loves us. Play music in the car or play it when you are doing chores around the house. Music is such a beautiful way to instill deep truths into our children's souls.

- *Read the Bible where and when your littles can see you.* When your children see you doing something, they will develop a curiosity about it, and when you are consistent, they will stash that in their brain as important. Read the Bible as you hold your kids. Show them your Bible. Read to them from a children's board book Bible. Help them to grow in their curiosity and love for God's story.

- *Listen to them intently.* Sometimes you may feel that your pre-verbal child is muttering mostly incomprehensible sounds. But imagine for a moment that they are telling you about Jesus in some way. Maybe they are! Listen to them in various times and spaces that help them feel as though there is nothing else going on in the whole world. Look them in the eyes. Get down at their level. Listen. Acknowledge. Encourage.

- *Tell them that you love them, and Jesus loves them, and show them that this is true.* You can show them in the consistency of your actions. You can show them in the way in which you embody and express the fruit of the Spirit in your life. You can show them each day in many different ways, and you can tell them each day too. My grandpa would always say, "Jesus loves you and so do I."

- *Introduce them to the body of Christ that is the church.* Do this in a way that is celebrative, consistent, and communal. Make your gathering times with the church community as natural as you can so that your child feels safe and peaceful about the experience. The body of Christ offers such an amazing extended family. For your little one to get to experience that wonderful aspect of Christianity right from the start is a gift both to your child and to your church community.

- *Practice gratitude.* While it may seem as though this was covered in the prayer point, the reality is that gratitude goes beyond prayer. Gratitude to God in prayer is one aspect of this, but gratitude to others in our journey is also an important practice. We may tell our little ones, "Say thank you!" but we often forget to say it ourselves. As we model thankful hearts, our children will come to know a world that is a blessing to us all. Gratitude, even in the small things, will help your child see the world in a different light.

10

LITTLE BLUE APRON: AGES TWO TO FIVE

Take chances, make mistakes, get messy!
—Ms. Frizzle

The developmental range of preschoolers is vast. There are two-year-olds who speak in full sentences and two-year-olds who only have a handful of words. There are three-year-olds who are beginning to recognize some letters and three-year-olds who are content to eat sand. There are four-year-olds who can navigate a computer as well as their grandparents and four-year-olds who cannot sit still long enough to watch an episode of *Sesame Street*.

While there is a vast range of physical, emotional, and intellectual development, I believe this is also true for spiritual development. Some children will really engage in worship at this age, some will love to pray, and others will soak up the story of Scripture. But not all children will desire or focus on the same areas at the same time. Regardless of the diversity in spiritual development throughout this stage, children are developing in their awareness of God. In fact, most children develop an elementary understanding of who God is by age five.[1] When we shape that understanding through story, practices, and consistency, and in other practical ways, we help young children to know and believe that Jesus is what God looks like. In this way, we are setting them up with the most solid of foundations. As we do this, God works in children in amazing ways—ways that we adults often overlook.

When my daughter was about three and a half, we were driving somewhere, and she had been singing and chatting, and then for a few moments was completely silent. I thought she had fallen asleep. I looked back in the rearview mirror. She hadn't fallen asleep at all. She soon took a deep sigh and said as she looked out the window, "It's all so beautiful, isn't it?"

I said, "What are you looking at, kiddo?"

She replied, "Just the world, Mom."

We were both silent for a moment. "Let's thank God for it," I added.

"Okay, Mom. God, thank you for your good world," she prayed.

Amen. Amen.

Preschoolers need downtime to process, to think, to allow their rapidly growing brains to catch up. (Actually, all of us need it!) During this downtime they will formulate questions and ideas about the world, including the spiritual world. Just as we as adults find particular kinds of quiet time suited to our personalities, each preschooler's quiet time may look different. Some may need to be on the move to process their thoughts. Some may need to stare out a window. Some may need to color a picture. All these things are done best without additional external stimulus.

There is a difference between *quiet* downtime and *together* downtime. Together downtime may look like reading a book together or telling a preschooler a story. Rachel Held Evans writes in *Inspired*: "Researchers tell us one of the greatest gifts we can give our children is the ability to tell stories. Helping them apply narrative to their everyday experiences, and to see a purpose and direction in the forces that shape their lives, improves both cognitive function and well-being. Recounting everything from a skinned knee to a school field trip to a traumatic event like a car accident or death in the family with the aid of storytelling helps children make sense of their fears and emotions and manage them in a healthy way."[2]

Clearly, Jesus was ahead of these researchers. He knew that the way in which we tell and receive stories matters greatly. It's no coincidence that Jesus used stories, called parables, to answer many of the questions he was asked. *Who is my neighbor? Let me tell you a story . . . What is the kingdom of heaven like? Let me tell you a story . . .*

Story really does help us make sense of life. Telling a story helps us to clarify our viewpoint of what we believe we have accomplished. Hearing a story helps us know and understand others' roles and how we are connected to the stories of others. Telling children stories from the Bible—and specifically helping them connect the biblical narrative with Jesus as the main character—helps them see that they, too, have a part in this big, beautiful story of God.

Our understanding of our role in God's story may not be apparent to preschoolers—although I wouldn't put it past any of them to figure it out. But as preschoolers hear God's story, as they listen to the Bible stories we read to them, they take in every word (and often tell you when you've missed one). When we plant in their hearts stories about Jesus, his birth, his life, his ministry, his mission, his stories, and finally, his death and resurrection, we plant a seed that has great potential of becoming a deeply rooted, sturdy tree with many wonderful branches. When we help our children fall in love with Jesus through their experience of God's story, we really are giving them the greatest gift.

I believe that our understanding of what role we play in God's story continues to be revealed throughout our lives. This concept may first start to be unpacked in this age and stage, but it continues throughout our lives. I know that is true for me, and it is probably true for you. One day, when my daughter was about four, I had a slight epiphany in this vein. Erin had developed an interest in baking. She really loved the idea of baking cakes and cupcakes. There was nothing else that could quench that burning desire in her to bake. I should tell you that baking is not really my forte. I've ruined multiple loaves of banana bread, and I'm told there is not much that is easier to bake. So when I tell you that my daughter wanted to bake with me, you can imagine how out of my element I felt. When you consider any task, and then add a kid's "help" to it—well, the task multiplies in magnitude and length by a factor of ten.

My daughter put on a little blue apron she had been given. She wanted to add each ingredient to the bowl, and she did so as carefully as she knew how (ahem . . . she didn't really know how). Oh, and she wanted to stir. All the powdery ingredients. The powdery ingredients that would end up in various nooks and crannies in my kitchen. I aged years as she stirred.

But then two things happened at almost the same time. The first is that I began to really enjoy this baking endeavor with my kid. I couldn't believe it, but the slow-motion mixing and the random powder disbursement no longer bothered me but delighted me. This messy, wonderful experience with my child was bringing joy to my heart.

And then the second thing hit me: God loves to work with us, his kids, just as I was delighted to work with my daughter. God, the creator of the universe, bakes with us. Every day. God does this when he chooses to work with us to build his kingdom. It's shocking, really, but it is also so very cool. God is the master baker, and we are the four-year-olds with our little blue aprons. The lesson I was taught that day will not soon be forgotten.

Throughout this age of growth and experience, preschool children watch and learn a great deal from those with whom they spend their time. They begin to say the small phrases that we use. Hearing a child imitate our diction can be hilarious. Sometimes it can be alarming.

Considering this, we really do need to lean into Jesus more and more each day. Children choose to imitate us. We must choose to imitate Christ. We can bring our children, in short spurts, into our spiritual practices at this age.

Here are some concrete, put-faith-into-action suggestions for you to consider as you engage with your blossoming little disciple.

~~DON'T~~ TRY THIS AT HOME

- *Model the spiritual practice of quiet time for your children.* I cannot remember who told me about this idea. (If you are my friend and it was you, I want to buy you a coffee to thank you.) My friend shared about how she spends her own quiet time with Jesus while her preschoolers are at home. She lights a candle for half an hour each day. While the candle is lit, the children know that they are not to disturb Mommy while she spends time with Jesus. Should a child say that they want to spend time with Jesus too, she offers them some way of spending quiet time: a children's Bible, a coloring sheet, a ball of yarn. If any of the children are not interested in having quiet time, they are not forced into it at all. But it remains a time for the parent to have quiet time with Jesus: half an hour of a candle lit. When it's blown out, chaos, once again, may ensue.

I love this idea for many reasons. First, many parents talk about how difficult it is to spend time alone with Jesus while they have little ones. This scenario—in which children are invited to join if they'd like—makes it possible to do just that. Second, it models for a child the importance of reading the Bible or praying in everyday life. Third, devoting half an hour each day to some type of quiet time for at least the parent serves to slow down the pace of the day for a parent and child. In a culture that never stops, such modeling is a gift.

- *Read the Bible where your child can see you.* When your children see you do something, they will often develop a curiosity about it. When you are consistent in a practice, they will stash that away in their brain as something that is important. Show them your Bible. Read to them from a children's Bible and other children's storybooks about Jesus. This is such a fun age and stage for kids to engage with stories. Help them to grow in their curiosity and love for God's story by reading to them often. And again: Be ready for all the repetition. You are in the prime stages of repetition as a love language! Read and read again.

- *Pray with your child.* Jump back to page 124 to review the prayer ideas for younger children (in fact, you may want to keep your thumb there for a few moments!). Continue to build on these ideas with your child in this stage. Slowly and surely, you'll be able to encourage them to do more of the talking to God and you'll do less on their behalf. While being consistent with prayer times, you may find it helpful to diversify how you do your prayers. Create prayer sticks: Write people's names on craft sticks and put them in a jar. At prayer time, pull them out one at a time to pray for those people. Create a prayer tree or prayer wall: Write prayer requests or answered prayers or people to pray for on cutout leaves or sticky notes and attach them to a wall in your home. Choose to filter through a few prayers per day, or add answered prayers to the wall, or both. Have your child choose a few to pray for or give thanks for. Go for a prayer walk: Take a walk together outdoors and thank God for all the wonderful things you see.

- *Embrace musical worship.* Sing songs and hymns. Worship Jesus through music. Similar to the younger age category, I strongly suggest finding Jesus-centered tunes that your child will enjoy so that they can experience musical worship at their own level. I know that sometimes these are not parental favorites, as they're often the type of songs that get stuck in your head for all eternity. So also play the worship music that you enjoy.

Help your child discover that musical worship can feel and sound like many different things. Some kids really resonate with musical worship and will be drawn into the time of worship. Help them learn that the focus is on Jesus and how much we love him. As we worship, we focus our hearts on him.

- *Listen intently to your child and help your child learn to listen to you and others—including God.* I mentioned this in the previous chapter as well, but in our day and age, I think it bears repeating. (Heaven knows I need to remind myself!) Get at eye level with your child and *really* listen. Put down your phone. (That one in particular is for me.) Take time to really lean in and listen. Go out for hot chocolate and talk. Take some play dough or coloring pages and use the tactile experience while you talk. Your child will stay engaged longer. Kids are dying to be heard—really *heard*—by the adults who love them. Be the adult to listen, acknowledge, and encourage them.

- *Tell them that you love them, and Jesus loves them, and show them that this is true.* Again, this was mentioned in the previous chapter, and will be true throughout their lives, but it is something that many of us need to be reminded of often. Tell them you love them, tell them Jesus loves them, and let them know nothing will change that. And embody that love for them each and every day.

- *Engage with them in the body of Christ that is the church.* This was also mentioned in the previous chapter, and depending on where you are in your spiritual journey and the age of your child, this may be a helpful prompt to you: go to church gatherings together, go regularly, and celebrate the gathering time as a positive experience. Not only is it healthy for your child's spiritual development (and your own!); it is also such a gift to the body of Christ that is the church to see children at church gatherings. Children bring life in an unparalleled way.

- *Practice gratitude with your child.* Thumb back to the last chapter first, and then we'll build off that. It's okay, I'll wait. Okay, from there, as we model thankful hearts, our children will come to know a world that is a blessing to us all. We can do this by practicing gratitude in the ups and downs of life. When life is good, and everything is fine, thank God. When life is rotten, and things feel chaotic, thank God anyway. Gratitude is a spiritual practice that kids, and hey, most adults, may not realize the importance of, but gratitude really does change our mind-set. It makes us feel better. It improves our physical health. There is a reason why Paul instructs the church at Philippi, "Always be full of joy in the Lord. I say it again—rejoice!" (Philippians 4:4). This is good for us. It helps us refocus on God and takes the focus off ourselves.

  There is no end to how we can exercise our gratitude muscles, but one practical way to do this is to help your child choose one person each week to create a special thank you card for, and deliver it to that person. If you really want to go the extra mile, you could also add in some baked goods. Children will also see the impact that their gratitude can have on others, which is a bonus by-product of gratitude!

- *Remind your child that they are not alone.* Somewhere between the ages of two and a half and three and a half, children begin to experience concrete fears. They become much more aware of things in the world that make them afraid. When they are afraid or when life seems uncertain, help them know that you are with them and that God is with them. Remind them that Jesus loves them. Even if it *feels* as if they are alone, let them know that they are not. Reassure them and help them feel secure.

- *Serve together.* This one may seem almost impossible. How could you possibly serve with a child this age? You probably can't, *really*. You can probably only half serve. But the long-term payoff is so good. There are nonprofit organizations that will allow young children to come with their parents to serve that also have serving opportunities suitable to small children. A few ideas include unloading boxes at a local food bank, packing school kits for an international aid organization, and helping to clean service areas at local nonprofits. (My caveat here would be to ensure that, even with your little one, you are actually helping more than hindering. We can have the best of intentions, but still cause unnecessary frustration for the staff or organization if our "helping" isn't actually helping at all.) There are also informal ways to serve with your little one, such as preparing a meal for an elderly member of your neighborhood and delivering it together, or having your little one create a piece of artwork to take to someone you know who is sick in the hospital, or baking some cookies together and delivering them to a local first responders unit.

Depending on where you are or what you are doing, your child may limit your overall ability to serve as you try to scramble to help them focus, do, or redo their task. That being said, the benefit is that your child develops a heart and understanding for service. Depending on for whom and where you serve, you may also discover that children break the ice with people who may be more difficult to try to get to know as adults. When we help our children experience serving regularly while they are young and establish it as a meaningful part of their lives, it may well continue as they grow up. All of this makes it well worth the half service you might be able to do when they are young.

11

COLORING THEIR WORLD: AGES SIX TO TEN

Children are likely to live up to what you believe of them.
—Lady Bird Johnson

As children enter their school-age years, they become more independent and explore the things, ideas, and personal preferences that make them a fully rounded human being. And the same is true for their spiritual growth. Children will develop a greater appreciation for one spiritual practice over another, or a certain style of worship over another. Each child will grow spiritually, that is, grow closer to Jesus, in different ways. The opportunity presented to us, as parents and mentors and pastors, is to help them discover the points of spiritual connection that really resonate with them. While children are discovering the best ways that they learn (with a variety of learning styles to consider: visual, verbal, aural,

physical, and so on), they can also explore the most meaningful ways to connect with God.

In his book *Sacred Pathways*, Gary Thomas describes nine
spiritual styles. A spiritual style is how someone experiences
or connects with God. The nine pathways, or styles, that
Thomas outlines are as follows: naturalists (those who love
God out of doors), sensates (those who love God with their
senses), traditionalists (those who love God through ritual
and symbol), ascetics (those who love God in solitude and
simplicity), activists (those who love God through confrontation), caregivers (those who love God by loving others),
enthusiasts (those who love God with mystery and celebration), contemplatives (those who love God through adora-
tion), and intellectuals (those who love God with the mind).[1]
I remember when I began to discover that there were a variety of ways to connect with God. It was as if my world went
from black, white, and shades of gray to beautiful colors
everywhere. As parents, we may be inclined toward a certain
pathway or style of experiencing God. Our kids, however,
may be activated and given life and connection to the Spirit
in a completely different way. What a gift it can be to help
our kids experience different spiritual styles so that they can
discover how they best connect to and relate with God. This
will help color their world.

When my daughter saw her Catholic cousin cross herself
after a prayer, my daughter was intrigued. Later, she asked
me what "that" was. I explained to her that making the sign
of the cross is a way to physically remind ourselves of God
as Father, Son, and Holy Spirit. My daughter loved it! She
thought this was such a wonderful thing. "Can I do that?"
she asked. I said that of course she could.

Is my daughter a traditionalist? Maybe. I'm not inclined to stick a label on her, and I don't think that's the important part of understanding spiritual styles. Rather, knowing that there are different ways to connect with and relate to God is the best takeaway of the nine sacred pathways. While our kids are young, they may find certain spiritual practices boring or difficult, but they may fall in love with others. As spiritual parents committed to raising disciples, we can help them explore spiritual styles so that they can find moments of deep meaning with God.

As our children are further discovering who God is and how they relate to God's story, they may begin relating to peers from other religious traditions. As a result, children may come home with big questions about why some people believe different things than they do, or how the Bible is different from another holy book, or why we follow Jesus and not Muhammad or Buddha or Vishnu. They will begin to wonder about and express bigger thoughts about how we know what we know or what to say or do when someone challenges their belief systems. Don't let these things worry you. Embrace them. Let your child know that you don't actually know everything. They may be surprised at first, but it's a great lesson for them that no one does!

Also, commit to looking into the questions with your child. Is there someone else you know who has wisdom in that area? Go to them together to learn. Is there a great book or website that can help you both discover more? Check it out together. You can also let them know that many Christians who are wonderful hold different views from other Christians who are also wonderful. This is a great big lesson to learn, but one that is so meaningful to our lives long term.

Your child may ask certain questions that raise some insecurities in you—however, those may turn into a great exploration that may bring you and your child closer to Jesus.

When it comes to the application suggestions for this age category, I want to build off the previous application suggestions from the age before. I don't want to make things redundant, but I will add things in an age-appropriate way for you and your child to explore together.

~~DON'T~~ TRY THIS AT HOME

- *Sit with Jesus, and do so with your children.* It is common in many schools today to practice mindfulness with children this age. The idea is to allow children processing time—a chance to return their mind to a gentler pace. Mindfulness helps the overall health and well-being of a child. That being said, mindfulness is only a partial win here. When we take the idea of mindfulness and meld it with focusing on Jesus, we get something akin to centering prayer. When my daughter and I do this, we call it "sitting with Jesus." We simply close our eyes, take deep breaths, and imagine sitting with Jesus. My daughter and I really do allow the Holy Spirit to take over our imaginations. In doing so, we've even been transported in our minds to flower-filled fields to sit with Jesus as he invites us to come and rest. Sitting with Jesus, a type of mindfulness or meditation, is not something we do for hours. We do it for a few minutes—two, maybe three. When children are this age, learning to sit, and breathe, and focus on Jesus cannot be forced. We can invite our kids into this kind of practice, but we cannot push them. They will easily resent it and become uninterested. If your child has been invited and doesn't show interest, simply practice this yourself and share about your experience. Invite them into your practice occasionally. But if they are not interested, this simply may not be a way in which they connect with Jesus.

- *Read the Bible with your child.* In this age range, as your child develops in their own ability to read, create a special moment in giving them their first full-length Bible. Write their name and a special dedication inside the Bible along with the date, so that they know this is an important life event. Give it to them at a special dinner or before they head off to camp for the first time or at another occasion that will be memorable to them. Help your child learn how to navigate the Bible. Teach simple navigation techniques, such as where the table of contents is and what it is, how to find a book of the Bible, and that the big numbers on the page are the chapters and the little numbers are verses. All these things are beneficial for your child to learn at this age and stage. You can make a game out of it as you challenge one another to find passages in the Bible. If you grew up in a church, you may have done "sword drills," a game in which all participants hold their closed Bibles up in the air, someone calls out a passage, and everyone races to look it up. While I joke about many of the things I learned growing up, and while sword drills have become an easy target for adults reflecting on their fundamentalist Christian upbringing, I've got to tell you: I absolutely love sword drills. And you know what they say: what was old is new again.

Another way to help your child learn their way around the Bible was also prevalent in many a Sunday school class of my childhood: a song about the books of the Bible. To this day, I find myself singing the-books-of-the-Bible-in-order song I learned as a child to find some of the Minor Prophets. This is also a great stage to begin to introduce your kids to some of the lesser known but oh so interesting Bible stories: Balaam's donkey, the healing of Naaman, or young King Josiah. Help them fall in love with God's story.

- *Pray.* Suggestions for praying with children in the previous chapters included ideas for praying in fairly simple forms. Introducing new prayer forms to our children throughout this stage will allow them to discover how they best connect with Jesus, and they will learn that there are so many different ways to pray. They will learn that prayer doesn't have to be boring! This stage, when children are between ages six and ten, is a time when kids can try out additional prayer styles: prayer journaling, praying while creating art, praying the ancient prayers of the church by memory. There are five-finger prayers, in which each finger represents a person or group of people to pray for. There are so many ways to pray, and this is a great stage in which children can learn that truth.

In our discipleship journey, prayer is a huge part of the transformation process. While we might not always like to pray in a certain way, there is such a variety in how we can approach prayer. Let's help our children see that they can approach prayer like a buffet table: they can try a little bit of traditional prayers (for example, the Lord's Prayer) at one point in the day, and then simple sentence prayers or journaling at other points in the day.

- *Engage in musical worship: sing songs and hymns and worship Jesus.* Kids will start to mature in their musical tastes, and the Jesus-y tunes from children's music collections may not cut it as children grow older. They will want something that matches their growth and maturity. Take the time to discover some worship music that your child enjoys. Continue to sprinkle in additional worship music that isn't entirely their preference so that they can learn to appreciate the diversity in how people worship Jesus. This may include a vast array of styles, from Latin American Christian music to a children's choir from Botswana to Byzantine chants. As a kid, I remember watching the Gaithers on television with my grandparents. If you don't know who the Gaithers are, be sure to look them up online just to get a glimpse! They definitely weren't my "brand" of music then, but I actually grew to enjoy the variety of musical worship that they brought to the stage. My guilty pleasure now is listening to the Gaithers' Homecoming series. I think it reminds me of my grandparents, who passed away long ago.

Find out what it is that your child likes as far as worship music. Talk about what certain phrases mean and why they are in songs. Sometimes providing clarity and simple explanations for your children can go a long way. I remember discovering that my daughter loved the song *My Lighthouse* by Rend Collective and hearing her sing it over and over again. I wondered if she knew what the symbolism in the song meant, and as I had just begun to explain, I was cut off by her explanation to me: "Mom, Jesus is our lighthouse, and when we don't know where to go or what to do when life is hard, he helps us find our way." Uh, yeah, that about sums it up. Who said six-year-olds couldn't think in the abstract?

- *Listen.* Increase your time and space for quality listening. Face-to-face time is great, but some kids may actually share more openly with you when they have "shoulder to shoulder" time: time and space when you are doing something creative or constructive, or when you are playing a game with them (whether a board game or video game), or even while driving in the car. Depending on how your child is wired, you may need to prompt or lead the conversation. If your child is a natural sharer, you may just need to give them the space and they will begin to talk or ask questions and allow the conversation to flow from there. Or perhaps your child is not the talkative type, and you may need to prompt by asking questions or sharing something about yourself (a story from when you were that age) to begin a conversation and check in on where they are at in their thinking. If your child really loathes conversation, or just really struggles with it, you could make space for listening and sharing through reading and writing. Consider buying a special journal just for you and your child in which you write a note to them about something, such as your questions about God when you were their age, and you ask them what they think about those things and allow them to reply in their own time.

- *Continue to tell your kids regularly that you love them and that Jesus loves them, and show them that this is true.* As your child ages, your consistency in showing love becomes increasingly important. In Gary Chapman and Ross Campbell's book, *The Five Love Languages for Children*, they outline how the five "love languages"—physical touch, words of affirmation, quality time, gifts, and acts of service—connect with children. As you learn the most effective ways in which your child receives love, you can help your child feel truly known and loved in that way. And it's important to remember that our kids may not receive love the same way we do.

- *Be active in the church.* Go together, go regularly, serve together at church, and celebrate the gathering. Encourage your child to make connections with other kids at church, invite those kids over to play, and help cultivate your child's experience of church community. Get to know your child's children's ministry leaders and make meaningful connections with them. Thank them, pray for them, encourage them. Consider inviting them over for lunch! Be aware of what your kids are learning and experiencing in their children's church time so that you can talk about it with them.

- *Practice gratitude with your child.* Continue to build off the practices of gratitude mentioned in the previous age categories. Encourage your child when they express interest in thanking someone or showing appreciation in some way. Consider creating gratitude lists naming whom and what you are thankful for and why. Make notes of thanks to God and post them around your home. As you see these notes, take time to speak words of thanks to God.

- *Remind your child that they are not alone.* Depending on the temperament and personality of your child, fear of being alone may continue to plague them through these years. Letting your child know that you are there for them and that you want to support them may not seem like a spiritual practice, but it sure may feel like one to your child.

- *Serve together.* Serving together is an excellent opportunity to get some of that "shoulder to shoulder" time while living out what God calls us to do: feeding, clothing, and serving the poor and disenfranchised. It may seem as though many agencies will not allow children to serve; however, keep on searching. Community organizations and church-related nonprofits often have certain jobs or opportunities that allow children to be involved. However, serving doesn't have to be done in an official way for it to be meaningful. Consider who the older adults are in your congregation and go visit them, or connect with a local seniors' residence. If your child is theatrical, encourage them to create a show to share with that person. If your child is musical, encourage your child to prepare a couple of songs to perform. If your child enjoys a certain game, encourage them to bring that game and teach the person you are visiting. Serving others is at the heart of who Jesus is. As we help our children discover all of who Jesus is, we can point them to Jesus washing his disciples' feet. We can model practical, contemporary ways to wash others' feet, and we can invite our children into the practice with us.

- *Send your kids to a Christian camp.* This may appear to be the antithesis of most of the things I advocate for. Sending your kids to camp could fit the let-other-people-disciple-your-kids approach that I've criticized in this book. But I genuinely believe that in sending your kids to a Christian camp, you are giving them multiple gifts. First, at camp, kids are moved away from the distractions of everyday life. This in and of itself is a gift to them; it allows them to take a breath from the frenzy of society. It can also open the door to space for transformation to happen. Second, they are being immersed in Christian community. I truly believe that going to camp, and being in Christian community in this way, is the closest opportunity our kids can get to having the type of community that the early church experienced. Third, at camp they are surrounded by fun-loving, Christ-centered counselors and staff who are keen on mentoring your kid. Fourth, children experience being away from home in a nourishing environment. Fifth . . . well, I could keep going, but for your sake, I'll stop there.

  I do realize that Christian camp can be costly. But every camp that I am connected with offers very generous scholarships and creates ways to make camp affordable. And in truth, many of us will spend money on sports, music lessons, art classes, and so on. It's true that camp is expensive, but sometimes (not always!) it's more about how we prioritize the resources we have. And of course, camp may not be good for all kids; some kids may not be cut out for this type of weeklong group experience. You know your kid; trust your gut.

During this season of life, kids are entering a time of unfettered chaos. With hormones pumping, their bodies are changing in new and strange ways as they begin a significant pursuit of who they really are. They are in search of their identity.

If there is one word I would use to focus on for the next three to ten years of a child's life, it is *identity*. With few exceptions, tweens struggle to know who they are as they desperately seek to fit in. Early adolescence is a time of being pushed and pulled in many directions while the body is doing all sorts of new things. I realize the term is overused, but the best word to describe this stage is, undoubtedly, *awkward*.

I vividly remember my own experience in this age bracket. I had, um, "blossomed" before many of my friends had, and I got glasses and braces in the same month. I had a thin white Bible that I brought to my public school each day. A layer of pimples coated my freckled face. During this season, my brother and I actually took first and second place in a "freckle face" contest. So life wasn't exactly pleasant. And I didn't even live in the era of the smartphone and social media. I cannot fathom the experience of today's middle schoolers, who are trying to discover who they are while being bombarded with contradictory messages from online and offline voices.

The added pressure of constant connection is certainly anxiety-inducing even to the most well-adjusted of adults. For kids in this stage, this stress can become crippling at times. Helping our kids develop a healthy balance of their online and offline experiences, as well as to feel secure in who they are, may require constant encouragement, support, and healthy boundary setting. Even if we have to be the "bad guy" sometimes. For our kids' spiritual health, as well as their mental health, helping them develop healthy habits around technology can feel like a constant battle, but it is one that is well worth the struggle. Technology is in no way our enemy, but our addiction to it is. As parents, leading by example is important. We can do this by not checking our phones at the dinner table or by ensuring our faces aren't constantly lit by a screen during hours when we are together with our families. These things aren't easy for any of us, but modeling a healthy relationship with technology is beneficial to our kids.

While our kids are wrestling with technology use during this time in their lives, it is vital to ask them about their online engagement. For kids, online engagement can feel more important than offline engagement when it comes to social interaction. Being left out, insulted, or hurt online can feel more painful than being left out in real social settings. As parents, we may experience a constant desire to rescue our children from these difficult situations. And while this may be needed at times, it is also essential that we, as parents, remember that learning to fall and rise up again are fundamental experiences for kids as they are maturing. These experiences help kids develop skills for healthy confrontation, problem-solving, and grit.

We know that learning to fail and recover is foundational for psychosocial development, but it is also true for spiritual development. Our children will also stumble in their faith and may struggle with it in this stage of life. And while it may be our impulse as parents to swoop in to attempt a rescue mission, it may be most beneficial for our children's spiritual development to allow them some time to struggle. Here I do not mean allowing our kids to free-fall; that's not good for anyone. But your child may be struggling in a healthy way, one that is helpful to development.

In fact, although it can be difficult for parents to see their children begin to question what they've been taught and perhaps even wrestle with their faith, this struggle is the very thing that will help those children solidify aspects of their faith in the long run. As in every other age category, middle schoolers can range in their experience of spiritual development, and so their questions and struggles will also vary. Some middle schoolers may begin to question the very images of God they have been presented with. Some may question creation or how we know we can trust the Bible. Some may wrestle with the violence in the Old Testament. Some may wrestle with how they see women treated in some churches. Some may struggle with how some Christians have treated people who are LGBTQ (lesbian, gay, bisexual, transgender, and queer). Some may begin to see hypocritical behaviors in the church that they hadn't noticed before.

There are many moving parts in this stage of development, and while as parents there is no way we can be prepared for them all, we can prepare for how we react and respond to our children's questioning. If we are to respond in an aggressive manner, our kids will immediately feel shut down. Practice a posture of calm receptivity, one that welcomes questions and curiosity. It will invite your child to come to you with these queries and thoughts.

I would suggest that there are two essential practices for parents in this stage. The first one I would wrap up in one word: *communication*. Allow children to come to you on their terms. Check in now and then. Try not to smother them, but let them know that you are there for them. Do what you can to create a safe and comfortable climate for your child to discuss any issue with you. Open communication builds trust. Trust builds respect. Mutual respect is healthy, and it's important at this age and stage. The second thing I highly recommend is prayer. Pray for your children's struggles. Pray for your own struggles with them struggling. Pray for other Christ-centered adults to come alongside your child. Pray that you would know how to best direct your child to Jesus. And if your children are open to it, pray with them, pray for them, pray over them.

With all these things in mind, the list of application suggestions at this stage leans on the respect factor. Almost all the suggestions in this chapter begin with the word *invite*. If a child feels forced into a faith commitment, it will become an obligatory experience instead of a meaningful one. And let's level for a moment: Jesus' love isn't coercive. Jesus invited others to follow him. He didn't force a single person. His love was invitational. We can follow in the way of Jesus by being invitational in our spiritual relationship with our children at this stage.

For parents who grew up in an obedience-based church culture (I see that hand), this can be a very difficult pill to swallow. Let's be honest: if your middle schooler asks you why they have to go to church, your first impulse might be to say, "We go to church on Sunday because that's what we do!" No questions asked. (How dare they question your good judgment!) But attending church is no longer the predominant cultural experience of our times. If their friends aren't going to church, your tween may begin to wonder why they should. If an experience isn't fun or meaningful, why do it? Preteens are already beginning to ask that question. Rather than panic because they're asking it, invite them to tell you more. Ask them how they would like to connect with God, or perhaps why that doesn't feel important to them right now. Tell them what church means to you, how gathering with your community of faith helps you orient yourself toward Jesus every week and reminds you who you are loyal to and who your people are, and why you desire that for your family.

Whether we should *make* our kids go to church if they don't want to at this stage is a messy conversation. I really don't think there is a one-size-fits-all answer. Some kids may put up a struggle about going to church, but get right into the midst of things once they get there and be completely content. That's most certainly a win. The nudge is needed, and the struggle is worth the gain. But other kids, after the battle to get them to a church gathering, have a horrible time while they are there. What is meant to encourage them spiritually and orient them toward Jesus becomes a soul-sucking experience. That's definitely not a win. This would be a time to meet your child where they are at on their journey. Ask questions about where they see and experience God in things. Ask them why they think things are a certain way or what they think God thinks about certain ideas. Seek their opinions on ideas about God that you have, and allow them to feel that they are meaningful contributors to the conversation. Respect will continue to grow.

Let me be clear, however: this is not an open invite to simply be your child's "friend" through this stage and peel back on parenting. That is not what I am intending at all. What I do mean is that if we have open dialogue with our kids and there is a healthy level of respect, then making space for them to consider their own spiritual journey and what they believe is quite necessary.

This may also be a time to explore a few different church communities together with your middle schooler. I'm not suggesting you "jump ship" from your church in a hasty manner. But if you see that your preteen will engage in another community when they are not engaging in your current one, I would suggest there could be a compromising win there. Perhaps your family "tries it out" for a season of time, or your middle schooler checks out the community's youth group in lieu of the Sunday morning gathering. The win is helping your child find a meaningful way to engage in the body of Christ during this age and stage.

~~DON'T~~ TRY THIS AT HOME

- *Invite your children to join you as you sit with Jesus, or simply prompt them to consider spending time with Jesus on their own.* As they are willing to listen, share your experience of this with them. For example, share how you interact with Jesus in these times, or what he is saying to you, or how you are feeling nudged to do something, or how your internal world feels more at peace.

- *Read the Bible and share with your child what you are reading.* Ask them if they'd like to read with you. Find a good, age-appropriate devotional guide to help them journey through something that helps them connect the dots in relevant ways.

- *Pray, and invite your tween to pray.* A lot. Your kid is navigating some troubling waters, but God is good. Ask, seek, knock. Let your child know, in as unpatronizing a way as possible, that you are praying for them. You could even ask them to pray for you in certain age-appropriate ways as well. Share with them about prayer experiences that have been meaningful for you.

- *Encourage engagement in musical worship: model it and equip your child for it.* Maybe you belt out Lauren Daigle as you drive in your car, or you've got your Hillsong playing while you work on a puzzle. Or perhaps you find some stillness in your house and listen to old hymns of the past. Help your child see that musical worship is a beautiful way to honor God. And invite your child to discover the wide breadth of musical worship genres that exist in the kingdom. Perhaps challenge your children to search for a style they didn't know existed or the song they like best and share it with your family.

- *Help your child think critically about media.* I realize that until now, most of the at-home application ideas have been primarily spiritual practices. This one may seem to deviate from that idea, but bear with me. For many middle schoolers, music is becoming increasingly important, and I don't mean hymns. The smorgasbord of musical options out there is unreal. Take some time to listen to what your tweens are listening to. Ask them why they like what they like and what the experience is that they are pursuing in that music. Talk about the lyrics and what they mean. Ask them if they believe the message they are hearing. Encourage them to hold that music up next to their own faith. How does it relate? Encourage? Discourage? By helping children become thoughtful consumers, you are helping them develop a level of discernment. In fact, this is a healthy practice for all the media your child may consume during this time: video games, movies, TV shows, YouTube content, social media accounts they follow. Encourage children to meaningfully consider the content they engage with. Depending on your children's level of spiritual development and maturity, a helpful boundary for them currently may be to ask them to consider: Does this music (or YouTube video or movie or video game) create a barrier to Jesus in any way? And, hey, they may ask you to consider the same about the media you are consuming, which may not be a bad idea either.

- *Listen.* Increase your time and space for quality listening. This may happen at the most inopportune times (see the next chapter). But I have gleaned from many other parents' experiences that it is critical to listen at whatever moments your tween chooses to talk with you. Take what you can get. Read between the lines. Draw your child close in this time of uncertain identity, and be an attentive parent who provides an anchor of support.

- *Continue to regularly tell your kids that you love them, and that Jesus loves them, and show them that this is true.* I said in the previous age category that your consistency becomes increasingly important as your child ages. I reiterate it here because I think it is that important. Help your children to see and know that whatever waves of life come their way, they can know that you love them, Jesus loves them, and nothing can change that.

- *Be active in the church.* Go together, go regularly, serve together at church as able, and celebrate the gathering time. If your church has a middle school ministry, connect your child with it. I cannot tell you how important I think this ministry is. In a season of life when your child is trying to figure out who they are, providing additional mentors in their life is invaluable. Sometimes, seeing that there are adults who are living a vibrant faith and active in "real world" experiences can be encouraging for middle schoolers in a way that primary caregivers may not be able to emphasize on their own. These adult mentors (or older teen mentors, or young adult mentors) are a gift to the kingdom family.

- *Practice gratitude toward your child.* This is a bit of a twist from prior age categories. But having known enough middle schoolers, I know how difficult it can be to practice gratitude toward some of them. (Disclaimer: I love middle schoolers. They are wonderful and bizarre and unique creatures. I am simply stating a truth based on science: middle schoolers are sometimes tough to love. Science.) Find moments when you are truly thankful for them, and let them know it. Ruminate on the things that you are grateful for about your child. Thank God for those things. Find new things. Absorb those moments.

- *Remind your child that they are not alone.* The middle school years can feel like the loneliest time in life. As your child's identity is floating and in flux, it can seem to them that absolutely no one understands them. You don't have to pretend you understand them, but let them know that they are not alone. Take time to speak into your child's life by highlighting the gifts, skills, talents, and uniqueness that your child displays. Write them a letter to cement these thoughts in their mind.

Offer support to encourage them with their goals. Help your child know that they are supported, loved, known, and not alone. Never alone.

- *Invite your tween to serve with you.* If service has been a part of your family for some time, this may not be so much an "invitation" as an obligatory thing; it's just something your family does. If that is your family, talk with your children about how they feel about what your family does. Ask for suggestions or ideas. As your child is maturing, help them feel that they have a voice to speak into certain family decisions in a way that helps your child realize they have an important role to play in the family too.

- *Send your kid to a Christian camp.* I do believe I made a solid case for that in the previous age category. But I will add: Christ-centered mentors speaking into your child's life, in a less complicated environment than your child is used to, creates the possibility for great growth and transformation.

13

FINDING GRACE: AGES FOURTEEN TO EIGHTEEN

Some days, doing the best we can may still fall short of what we would like to be able to do, but life isn't perfect on any front—and doing what we can with what we have is the most we should expect of ourselves or anyone else.
—Mr. Rogers

What began as squeaky voices and new (horrific) smells in middle school takes on all new forms in the high school years. Many kids have transitioned from their childhood bodies into full-on adolescence. As the external changes continue, the internal quest for identity becomes more urgent, more pressing. And while teens are trying to establish who they are, it can seem as if there are many different voices yelling at them about who they are supposed to be. They have peers bringing their preferences, ideologies, and baggage to the table. They have teachers and coaches bringing their preferences, ideologies, and baggage to the table. They have celebrities bringing their preferences, ideologies, and baggage to the table. They have us, as parents, bringing . . . well, all our "stuff" to the table. There is an onslaught of expectations from every angle. Do you remember the confusion and messiness of your teenage years? I sure do.

Teens today have the added pressure of feeling as though they have to be constantly connected or else miss out on something of extreme importance. They also have unfiltered access to information on basically everything. The judgmental eye of peers and strangers on social media weighs on them— all during a stage in life in which they actually lack the ability to make decisions with long-term consequences in mind.

I recently reread some of my diaries from my teenage years, and I am so thankful that I did not have social media at that stage. I am certain I would have felt left out of whatever fun everyone else was having, not to mention that I certainly would have posted some unfortunate pictures and probably poems. I am also thankful that I wasn't constantly wired; I never would have slept. As for the access to information, I must say that would have helped some and hindered some. I know that if I had been a teenager fifteen years later than I was one (whoa, that's a little *Back to the Future* sounding!), my life may have turned out much differently. My faith journey may have taken different turns. The constant connection to friends may have caused me more intense levels of anxiety than I already experienced.

So today, as we parent and mentor and minister to our teenagers, we must have so much grace. And then we must

pray for more grace. We must have a gentle and calm connection. We must guide teens in setting good boundaries for
themselves, and we must be willing to step in to set boundaries when they are unable or unwilling to do so. For example,
limiting screen time and not allowing phones in bedrooms
after certain hours may rub your teens the wrong way, but
may actually allow them to find healthier sleeping patterns
and permit their brains to take a break. And the boundary
discussion does not end with screen time. Teens at this stage
are testing boundaries and finding where they can push and
where they really need you to push back. These boundaries
may include what nights of the week they can go out with
friends, curfews, prioritization of schoolwork, and what
you believe healthy relationships look like. To do this well,
I believe we must spend time in God's presence so that our
lives in general and our relationships with our kids in particular overflow with the fruit of the Spirit.

We must also have grace for ourselves as we care for our
adolescents. I hear over and over again that parenting teenagers isn't easy. As a former youth pastor, I can safely say
that's an understatement. We will make mistakes. Sometimes
we will speak when we should be silent, and other times we
will be silent when we should speak. Sometimes we will be
too strict, other times too lenient. As a teen, I used to tell my
mom, "When you think you are helping, you aren't helping!"
(Yes, I could be a jerk teenager at times.) Unfortunately, there
is no "best way" to parent a teen, and there are no road maps
to make it easier. Every teen is different, and navigating the
difficult terrain is, well, difficult. Just as we give our kids permission to fail, we need to give ourselves permission to fail
(can I get an amen?). We must have grace for ourselves and

our co-parent in these times. This is an essential truth in this stage of parenting teenagers.

A former student of mine, who was about fifteen at the time, once told me that he had stopped telling his parents things that were important to him because he feared their reaction. This wasn't because they were cruel or unkind to him, but rather because they jumped in too far to help. He felt smothered. After some discussion, I convinced him to share these concerns with his parents. His very goodhearted parents just wanted what was best for him, but they weren't allowing him to develop his own level of independence. He needed space to grow on his own, but really did want to share what he was discovering with his parents. After several discussions and a lot of prayer on all fronts, this teen was able to recommence sharing with his parents. And his parents needed to give grace to themselves as they navigated the difficult terrain of not overstepping their son's boundaries.

This overstepping may be something you run the risk of doing. Or perhaps you give your teens too *much* space, thus swinging the pendulum in the opposite direction to the point that they are craving your guidance and boundaries. (Please note that they will never tell you this is what they are craving.) Either way, caregivers of teens may always feel that they are doing a kind of dance to find the appropriate balance of law and love.

With all this in consideration, how do we continue to point our teens to Jesus through these sometimes rocky years? It is one thing if your children are sailing along in their faith journey, enjoy the church community, and engage in spiritual practices on their own or with your nudge. It is a completely different story if they are questioning their faith or have expressed the desire to walk away from it entirely. In truth, for individuals to genuinely come to own their faith, they need to question it. This is one major reason why I would encourage kids to wait until they are at least into their midteens before being baptized. Until then, their faith will be an echo of their parents' faith. They won't have had the opportunity to sincerely wrestle through and own their faith. Baptism is how we, as Christ-followers, and before all our friends and family, commit to following Jesus forever. Yes, we hope that the love and Christ-following our children do in their early years is retained throughout their lives. Yet the true, long-lasting commitment to Christ that is symbolized in baptism should, I believe, be paused until children have the capacity to make a decision that is genuinely their own. And not ours as parents.

I know there are many differing views on baptism, and I know that mine is just one. Yet the cognitive and spiritual development stages that we looked at in chapter 8 would support this view that teenagers are ready to wrestle with and then own their own faith. However, as mentioned previously, there is always room for the Holy Spirit. As spiritual parents, we can be sensitive to the work of the Spirit in our kids' lives. This work of the Spirit is essential to helping them feel that they are following Jesus authentically. That authenticity may mean baptism for your younger teen; then again, it may be for that teen to question or wrestle with their faith.

It can be painful to have a teen living at home who is questioning their faith, or poking at it, or resisting it. Yet it may be more beneficial, in the long term, than if they do this while away at college or on their own. I say this because, at home, they have the availability of an invested parent and the constant reminder of your love for them and the love of Christ. Once they leave home for school, work, or other involvements, this process becomes quite a bit muddier. Home offers stability in a world of many other destabilizing forces. Author and minister Gary Thomas writes, "Out of love for our children, we must become strong enough spiritually to watch them hurt, to see them become disappointed, to hear their cries."[1] Our spiritual strength can help support them in their spiritual weakness.

If your teen does stray from the faith, whether while living at home or after moving away, what to do then? As with every other aspect of parenting teens, there are no hard-and-fast rules, except maybe this one: communication is key. We need to take a posture of listening, *really* listening, to our kids. Keep the dialogue going. If they have been raised from early childhood to follow Jesus, then chances are that they have all the "head knowledge" that they think they need, and there is little we can say to change how they are feeling about their faith journey (or lack thereof) at this time. However, there is much to be said for "heart knowledge," and that comes from how we orient ourselves toward Jesus and how that informs our actions and our willingness to listen openly to our questioning kids. At this age, Jesus-centered parenting looks like this: "Be quick to listen, slow to speak, and slow to get angry" (James 1:19).

Parenting teens can be tricky and stressful. But can I also say that it can be fun? I think Jesus-centered parenting also looks a lot like enjoying your time together as a family. Play board games. Take road trips. Go bowling. Take a hike. Be spontaneous. Be together. As you do these things, you model a full life of love to your children.

When it comes to application suggestions for this stage of life, I have divided this list into two parts. Part A is for you as a parent no matter where your teens are on their spiritual path, and part B is for parents to engage in with teens who are presently journeying with Jesus.

~~DON'T~~ TRY THIS AT HOME

Part A: For you as a parent

- *Pray, pray, pray.* Yes, I know I have said this many times before, but I cannot possibly emphasize it enough. Going to the Father for help with our parenting is the very best advice I know how to give.
- *Listen without agenda.* Oh my, this is difficult. But when we do this for our kids, something amazing happens: we hear them, and they feel heard. And sometimes that is enough.
- *Be consistent in your spiritual journey.* Continue to attend and engage in your church regularly, even if your teen chooses not to attend with you. Your consistency will be an example for your child.

Part B: For you as parent with an engaged or interested teen

- *"Sit with Jesus" together or ask them if they've spent time with him lately.* Share your experience of this with them and ask them about their own experiences.
- *Journey with your teen through a devotional book, or take a deep dive together into a gospel book to study through the life and ministry of Jesus.* This is a fantastic way to foster your teen's spirituality while you are also being developed.

- *Pray together.* Encourage them in their prayer life individually. Introduce them to new spiritual practices and prayer forms (*lectio divina*, imaginative prayer, fasting, centering prayer). Buy them a prayer journal as a gift. Encourage whatever Christ-centered spiritual practice they latch onto.

- *Worship together.* Be willing to drive them to worship events, and help them prioritize these if they are interested in them.

- *Continue to regularly tell your teens that you love them, and that Jesus loves them, and show them that this is true.* These extra-big kids still need to see and know that whatever waves of life come their way, you love them, Jesus loves them, and nothing can change that.

- *Consider taking part in a church discipleship program or conference or workshop together.* Ask your teen if there is something in that regard which they would like to pursue, and then make it happen.

- *Encourage a practice of gratitude.* Challenge your teen to consider people and things each day that they are grateful for, and invite them to show their appreciation for those people. Provide them with some gift cards and a stash of appreciation cards so that they can give these to people as they feel so compelled. In your generosity, the door will be opened for them to show gratitude well, and this may also encourage them to (eventually) use their own funds to show appreciation to others as well.

- *Send your teen to a Christian camp or encourage and allow your teen to work at one.* I realize that many teens need to work in their summers to pay for postsecondary education. I am well aware of the incredible costs that students undertake. Yet I still believe that allowing teens to work at summer camp—whatever humble wages they earn—is an investment that cannot be measured.

14

OPEN ARMS: EMERGING ADULTHOOD AND BEYOND

I'm not lost, for I know where I am. But however, where I am may be lost.
—Winnie-the-Pooh

Young adults, millennials, Generation Z: they are all the target of so much criticism within our culture. I'm sure you've heard it all: "Young adults don't know how to work hard"; "Millennials can't afford rent, but they buy avocado toast"; "Generation Z doesn't know how to speak to people face-to-face." With all the criticism and so many generalizations, young adults still tend to find their own way. But that doesn't mean they don't need our support.

Throughout the young adult years, your children may choose to heavily deconstruct the faith that they believe they have inherited from you. That does not mean that they will throw it all away. They may appear to discard pieces for a time. They may choose to try out new forms or faith traditions, but I want to urge you to remain consistent.

As we spiritually parent young adults, one way we can support them is through prayer. Prayer reminds us that there is a much bigger picture than the one we can see, no matter where our children are in their spiritual journey. Another vital thing we can do as we spiritually parent young adults (besides pray persistently) is be authentic, consistent, and encouraging. We need to be like John the Baptist: just keep pointing to Jesus. This is our job from now until we leave this earth. In a world of so much darkness, we can help reorient others to the Light.

Whether the young adult in question is your own child or someone you are spiritually parenting or mentoring or investing in, give them support and allow them to share their heart with you without judgment. As they ask for advice or wisdom, give it freely, but don't push what they don't want. At this age, while many young adults from Christian homes want to know what is right, they also want to be able to explore. Be the one who is standing firmly on that straight path, waiting for them with the consistent love of Christ.

In Luke 15, Jesus tells the story of the lost son, more commonly called the prodigal son. *Prodigal* can mean different things: wasteful, extravagant, reckless. And while it's an apt word to describe the son, we could also describe the father in this way. The father is extravagant, wild, and reckless in the way he loves his son. In that sense, we could call this story the prodigal father. We can learn some excellent lessons from this father as we walk through the story in his sandals.

Once there was a man with two sons. The younger son told his dad that he wanted his share of his inheritance now, so his father divided his wealth between his sons. First thing to notice here: Did the father yell at his son and tell him he was being ridiculous and to go and get a haircut and get a real job? No. He was not that kind of dad. Instead, the father leaned into the desire of the son. He allowed the son to make adult decisions—even if they were the wrong ones—and to experience the reality and consequences of the decisions, all while loving his son deeply.

Then this younger son packed up and hit the road for a faraway place. In the story, we follow the son to his destination. He clearly had no financial management skills or impulse control, and he squandered his cash quickly. And while our focus is on the son during this time, I cannot help but consider the father. I imagine him continuing his daily routines, all the while praying steadfastly for his son. I imagine he prayed continually for both his sons. Consistent. Steadfast.

And then when the younger son hit rock bottom in the muck of a pigpen, he thought of his father's home. This wayward son realized that even his father's servants were treated well and were well-fed. He knew his father was consistent in this way. So the young man journeyed home to his father. He planned to apologize and beg his father to take him back in as a hired hand, because he felt so unworthy to be the man's son.

But the good father didn't settle for a hired hand. He knew there was nothing that could make him stop loving his son. In fact, while the son was still far off in the distance, the father saw him and, without lecture or guilt trip, ran to embrace him. He was filled with love and compassion. He was so joyous that his son had returned that he threw him an extravagant party.

I cannot help but consider that this good father did not finger-wag. He did not say, "I told you so." He did not lecture his son on the level of stupidity that he had embodied. Instead, he loved him. He welcomed him. He celebrated him. I picture Jesus here, welcoming the young children whose parents brought them to Jesus. This father was welcoming his son home in the same way: with open, loving arms. With all the grace and gentleness and warmth of a good father.

There are a vast number of lessons we can glean from this good father on parenting a young adult. First, he models what it looks like to lovingly let your kid fail. The younger son had to leave and come back so that he could journey through this stage and solidify his identity as the son of an ever-loving father. Like his older brother, he may have questioned whether his father even valued him. While it doesn't always take journeying away to discover this value, it seems as though the younger son learned this in spades that day.

The father did exactly what the son needed him to: he showed loving compassion and he celebrated his very existence. Unfortunately, many young adults may feel varying levels of worthlessness. They may feel that they are floating at this stage in life, and they need to know they still have a safe place where they can be embraced just as they are. When the father in the story embraces the son, he rejoices and calls for a party. Why? Because, he says, my son was dead and now he is alive.

I imagine that for a long time the father thought he had lost his son. He thought his son may have journeyed too far and would never return. For any parents reading this whose young adult child has seemed to stray from their faith, know that your child's story is nowhere close to being finished. Even though you may think that there has been an end, a spiritual death, what appears to be dead can, in the kingdom of God, still have life. That's the power of the Spirit. Even in pain, we can maintain a posture like that of the good, good father and hold our arms open wide.

A 2018 study published by the Evangelical Fellowship of Canada tackled many questions about the faith formation and experience of young adults. One of the results that the study found was this: "Warm relationships with parents who live out their faith are vital for faith formation."[1] Parents: even when it seems as if your influence no longer matters, hold the course. You do still matter to your young adults, and you matter deeply. But you've got to be sure that your child's faith community goes deeper than your own family, especially at this stage in life. The study suggests that "young adults need persisting communities of faithful adults, mentors and friends in their lives. When young adults move, it is vital that families, churches and ministries work to get them connected to new Christian communities in a timely manner."[2] Connect. Encourage your young adults to connect. Pray that they connect. Pray for a solid mentor and faith community for them. This is the stuff that helps them when they are trying to piece together all that they have deconstructed. These are the people who will help point them to Jesus when they need redirection.

As a parent of a young adult, or as someone who is involved in ministry to young adults, you may have a great many frustrations or anxieties around decisions that they make. You may think that they aren't actually listening. (Then again, they may think that you aren't listening to them either.) It can sometimes look as if they have no concept of what following Jesus even means.

But take heart: young adults are attempting to figure out a lived faith that, up until this time, has mostly been modeled to them in the home or at church. They are still finding their footing as to what this looks like for them in real time. As they move away, or are in a post–high school setting, or enter the workforce in some way, the question, "What does it look like to follow Jesus here?" becomes a little trickier for them to discern. Have patience. Have faith. Hold steady in prayer. And keep your arms ready and open wide.

WHEN YOUR KIDS BECOME PARENTS

If you're a grandparent reading this book, please know how wonderful you are. Thanks for taking this time to invest so meaningfully. Perhaps you're a grandparent who has the joy of watching your children love Jesus as they raise their children to love Jesus. What a gift! Continue to point your children and your grandchildren to Jesus each and every day.

That being said, there is one major thing I'm learning from trusted friends who are further along in their parenting journey than I am. Grandparents, let your kids parent their kids. Let *them* set the tone, make the rules, set the standard. If you want to know if it is okay to read Bible stories to your grandkids, ask your kids. If you want to know if it is okay to take your grandkids to church, ask your kids.

I have a growing body of anecdotal evidence that suggests that many families experience major conflict as a result of grandparents overstepping on matters of faith. Grandma,

Grandpa, Nana, Papa, Oma, Opa: I absolutely understand. You want the very best for your grandchildren, and you so deeply desire that they encounter Jesus and experience a community of faith committed to him. But the very best for your grandchildren is for you to stay in their lives and remain in relationship with your children. The focus of your role becomes prayer and modeling.

Pray for your kids (I guess that never ends). Pray for your grandkids. Continue to show your kids love and grace. Show your grandchildren love and grace. Don't be afraid to share about your experiences with Jesus and how Jesus influences your life, while at the same time being conscious of where your children are in their faith journey. That said, if your children are comfortable with you being an active discipler of your grandchildren, go for it. The application suggestions in this section will deviate a little from the other age categories, as we've now entered into slightly different territory.

~~DON'T~~ TRY THIS AT HOME
Part A: For parents of adults

- *Consistently let your children know that you are praying for them.* Ask how you can be praying for them. If they respond negatively to this sentiment, keep it to yourself. Pray without ceasing in the quiet of your time with God.

- *If you go to a different church than your children do, take a Sunday to attend with them at their church.* Look for the positive things to comment on, and avoid any judgments that may arise in you.

- *Check in on your child's spiritual journey.* Ask questions like, "What has God been saying to you lately?"

and "Where have you been seeing God at work?" If this is not well received, give your child space for emotions and feelings related to this. Give your child time, and reapproach the conversation only in a time and space that feels safe to you both.

Part B: For grandparents

- *Consistently let your children know that you are praying for them and their children.* Ask how you can be praying for them.
- *Create opportunities to share your family's spiritual legacy.* Think campfire stories meet an old-school testimony night!
- *If you go to a different church than your children do, take a Sunday to attend with them at their church.* Take another Sunday and ask your children if you can take your grandchildren to your church so they can see a different expression of the body of Christ. Oh, and maybe give parents a Saturday date night and take the grandchildren for a sleepover.
- *Encourage your children in their parenting.* Let them know you see their efforts and how they care for their kids. Consider writing them a letter or card to put the encouragement in ink.
- *Write a letter to your grandchildren and send it in the mail.* Consider sharing with them your favorite Bible story or Bible verse, or how you came to know Jesus.
- *Model love and grace.* Grandparents, as I've seen, can grow to be either older, wiser, and more gracious or older, grumpier, and more crotchety. Choose the first option.

- *Purchase children's Bibles or devotional books for special occasions.* Write a note inside for your grandchildren. It may be something that ends up with an even deeper meaning for them as they grow older.

15

BAD TIMING AND WHAT IFS

God has made everything beautiful for its own time. He has planted eternity in the human heart, but even so, people cannot see the whole scope of God's work from beginning to end.
—Ecclesiastes 3:11

I had an entire day just for writing. I don't get *entire* days to do anything. I had it booked into my calendar, and I was eagerly anticipating it. Then my brother called to let me know that he had tickets to a daylong event that he wanted to take his wife to and they needed a babysitter for their daughter and son.

Now, everything in me wanted to say no—not because I didn't want to hang out with my niece and nephew, but because a day to write is so rare. But my brother and his wife have had a tough couple of years because of health issues, and they get even fewer days to spend together than I get entire days to do what I'd like to do. So I said yes.

My niece, Sloane, is nine months younger—almost to the day—than my daughter. (My husband and I like to say that we inspired them to become parents.) My four-year-old nephew, Knox, acts as if he has just had several Pixy Stix and a case of Coke. I love them both.

Anyway, my entire day for ~~writing~~ hanging out with my niece and nephew came. We played some games and then went upstairs to help my nephew put on his pirate costume. While upstairs, I found my niece's Bible, and I asked the kids if they'd like me to read them a story and they could act it out. They loved the idea, and soon one story turned into one more and one more. They argued about who got to be Jesus in each story—no, the irony is not lost on me—and at about the half-hour mark, I asked them if they'd like to stop and go swimming. "No!" they both shouted back at me. "More Bible!"

I kid you not: we did this for an hour and ten minutes. My throat dry from narrating, I finally said, "We've got to stop reading the Bible or you won't get to go swimming today."

So we drove to a pool a little more than half an hour from their house, and my nephew fell asleep in the car. We had been listening to a kids' worship album, and when Knox fell asleep, I turned it down. When I did, my niece said, "Aunt Nat, will you turn it back up?" So I did. We sang worship music for the rest of our way to the pool.

THE BEST TIME TO RAISE DISCIPLES IS NOW

My anticipated day of writing was replaced by something much better. What I experienced wasn't just a wonderful day with my niece and nephew: it was a day spent raising disciples. That day I got to tap in as an adult who gets to nurture them in the way of Christ. Within the quantity of time I knew I'd spend with them that day, I was surprised by the quality time we spent with Jesus too. What a perfect example of what it looks like to experience a most wonderful thing at an unfortunate time. The writing I needed to do that day did not get done, but I traded something important, something good, for something so much better.

The chance to nurture young disciples does not always come at opportune moments. We cannot be too choosy about when or where we receive the gift of mentoring a young person or having spiritual conversations with kids. It is well worth almost any inconvenience to get to journey with our children in this way.

Whether it is a day suddenly usurped by caring for someone else's children or a moment in which you just don't feel like getting into a deep conversation with your own: know that a "better time" may never come. Prayerfully take each opportunity to raise young disciples as it comes. Ask the Lord for the strength you need to dig into it, and get to digging.

The inconvenient times, the difficult questions, the random thoughts shared at random times: these are worth it. They really are. They are the ways that you really get to know your child's heart. In my experience, things often come to the surface at inopportune times and places: while I'm putting my daughter to bed, while I'm in the shower, or while I am busily scurrying to get something done. Our children often need to process experiences from their day, and they don't necessarily control when those things surface: a friend at school having surgery, a fight in the cafeteria, a question about a difficult family relationship, or a racist message written on a friend's locker.

While these moments may not always feel like it, they are the very best ones. Conventional wisdom or exhaustion may make me want to say, "It's time to be done talking now and go to sleep," or "Please let me shower in peace?" But *kingdom* wisdom tells me to shut up and listen. Kingdom wisdom means leaning in to truly hear what big things our children are processing. I've learned that this is time that I must simply surrender to God to allow him to work in our conversation— even if it happens in the bathroom.

BUT WHAT IF . . . ?

Parenting is not only full of unpredictable timing; parenting is also full of what ifs and worst-case scenarios. My parenting brain can lead me into some dark places when it comes to what those worst-case scenarios can be. Honestly, I think I could compete rather doggedly in the what's-the-worst-thing-possible-that-could-happen-to-my-child games. I would probably even medal.

So when I hear questions from parents that begin "What if . . . ," I must admit that my brain has probably already traveled there. "What if?" questions are usually the ones that we allow our brains to conjure up out of fear. Most of the time they are not based on our own real-world experiences or events likely to occur. Instead, they are so deeply fear-based that despite the irrationality of them, they are hard to shake.

After speaking to parents or teaching a workshop, I often get asked these kind of "what if?" questions. What if my child asks me if I have ever (fill in the blank with immoral behavior)? What if my child continues to hate church as much as they hate the nursery? What if I'm too strict/not strict enough/ too loving/not loving enough?

None of those are bad questions. In fact, find me on social media and pose any of these questions to me, and I'll give you my best responses. But here are even deeper ones—the ones that keep us up at night: What if I don't have answers for all the questions about God that my children ask me? What if my kid ultimately walks away from Christian faith? What if I've done this whole parenting thing all wrong?

Let's look at these one by one. So you're not sure you have all the answers for the questions about Jesus and faith that your kids might ask you? Good. In fact, great! Go ahead and be honest about the fact that you don't have all the answers. Your kids will appreciate and value your honesty over the trite or made-up answers that you could offer in lieu of the truth. It's such a relief to not know everything, and it will teach your kids the incredible truth that it's okay for them to not know everything too. From that point, you can attempt to tell your children what you *do* know. "Hey, kiddo, what an impressive question! I have thought about that before too. I don't have a great answer, but here's what I know: Jesus loves us so much, and because of that I think that *maybe* . . ." Then give your best thoughts on the answer to the question.

Another important question is, What if my kid walks away from their faith? This is a very good question. It's a very hard question. We know that so many young people do, especially during their late teen or young adult years. It is a painful reality for many parents. While we can never know what will stick for our kids and what won't, we can help our kids build a strong foundation, we can pray for them no matter their status with Jesus, and we can also be aware that their story isn't complete. While there is no easy answer for this question, there is always prayer. And we can take our cues from the prodigal father: just keep loving our kids. I think one of the risks that some Christian parents run when their children walk away from the faith is to come on too strong and with a judgmental edge. All this will do for children who have already walked away from the faith is further ostracize them from family, which is perhaps the only touchpoint with Christ-followers they may encounter in their day-to-day lives. The father in the Luke 15 story reminds us that even if our children wander, we can be consistent in our love and embrace them with open arms.

A related question that I have received more than just a few times is not exactly a "what if?" It's the dreaded "What did I do wrong?" I usually hear this question from parents of youth or young adults who aren't currently in any form of relationship with Jesus. The reality for me is that I often have no idea what type of parent this person was or is, and I don't know if they screwed up seven ways from Sunday. But when they come to me with this question, I can tell it is often from a place of deep brokenness and heartbreak.

As such, the appropriate answer often looks something like this: We all do something wrong. Especially when it comes to parenting. None of us will do it perfectly; that's just how it goes. However, young adults have the world at their feet, and they have the ability to make their own choices in every avenue of life. That includes their faith. Should your child choose to leave the faith, or the church, or walk away from God, you must know—and please hear me on this—this is not the result of a mistake that you've made. Regardless of whether your child has been given a solid foundation, children have the ability to choose their every step at this point, and we cannot make them choose Jesus. That's not how this all works.

That being said, when parents ask, "What did I do wrong?" they are demonstrating that they still care about their child's walk with Jesus. And while that child may not be serving Jesus right now, I often remind parents that their child's story is not done. And when I don't have much more wisdom flowing from the Holy Spirit than that, I pray. I don't have answers to everything, but I always have access to the One with the answers.

Another question in the good-but-hard category is, What if my child is let down by our church community? Sadly, this is almost a guarantee. I mean, church communities are filled with people, messy people. Just like me. And while it is my hope and prayer that I don't let people down, especially young people, I know I will, and I have. And although that may be the case, I don't think that is a complete and utter tragedy. I think it is an opportunity for our sons and daughters to learn valuable lessons about what it looks like to keep going when things get tough, and still cling to a church community. What does it look like to continue to be the church when we are awakened to the reality that the church is messy? It looks like family.

Having said this, I am referring to times that our children are met with hypocrisy in the church or gossip or people being generally mean or rude. It is an entirely different story if our children are abused in any way: physically, sexually, emotionally, or spiritually, especially by church leadership. If that is the case, do what is needed to protect your child and other children, whether that involves reporting abuse to law enforcement, finding a church community or space that feels safe to your child as they heal, and so forth.

There are many big, weighty "what if?" questions. These are but a sampling. But without sounding trite, I would say that 100 percent of the time, the answer begins with prayer. I pray. I invite others to pray with me. We will, at times, fast and pray. We pray, "Let your will be done on earth as it is in heaven."

~~DON'T~~ TRY THIS AT HOME

- When do your children process their day? What is one way you can make space to do this in a way that enables both or all of you to be in your best zones?
- Find a quiet moment and write out your worst-case scenarios or big "what if?" questions. Share them with a trusted spiritual friend and pray through them together.

16

WHAT'S THE MOST IMPORTANT THING AGAIN?

When the kingdom of God shows up, kids learn what God is like by looking at their parents. And now God's will is being done in the family as it is in heaven.
—Gregory Boyd

A lot of noise and expectations are thrown at parents in every stage of their parenting journey. Parenting can lead us into some terrible places and can draw out of us some of our worst fears, anxieties, and behaviors. But as we continue to focus on Jesus each day, we are reminded of his love, grace, wisdom, and peace. When we live each day with the awareness that Jesus is the most important thing in our lives, and when we orient ourselves in this way, the perfect love of Christ can cast out the fear that is prevalent in parenting. We haven't been given a "spirit of fear and timidity, but of power [and] love" (2 Timothy 1:7). We have all that we need to parent our kids in the way of Jesus and raise disciples, because we have Jesus as our focus and the Spirit within us. We just need to keep authentically pointing our kids to Jesus. That is the best and most important thing we can do. Our hearts, and the good Father's heart, are for our kids.

In Luke 1, we encounter the priest Zechariah and his wife, Elizabeth, two incredible and righteous individuals who desperately desire a child of their own. They meticulously obeyed the law. And while Zechariah was conducting his priestly duty, he was chosen to enter the sanctuary of the Lord and burn incense. A crowd stood outside and prayed. While Zechariah was in there, an angel came to him, and Zechariah was pretty freaked out. The angel said, "Don't be afraid! God has heard your prayer. Your wife will have a son, and you are to name him John." The angel went on to tell Zechariah what John would be like, and what John would do. And the angel also said this: "He will prepare the people for the coming of the Lord. He will turn the hearts of the fathers to their children, and he will cause those who are rebellious to accept the wisdom of the godly" (Luke 1:17). Zechariah didn't believe the angel, and was silenced until his son was born. Like, literally silenced: he couldn't speak.

With so much going on in the story, it can be easy to gloss over this phrase: *He will turn the hearts of the fathers to their children.* This was first highlighted for me by Greg Boyd, teaching pastor at Woodland Hills Church. Luke was quoting from Malachi 4:6, which describes the Elijah figure that will come before the Christ: "His preaching will turn the hearts of fathers to their children, and the hearts of children to their fathers." The prompt of John the Baptist in preparing the hearts of people for Christ will be so life-altering that the hearts of fathers (and all parents, actually) will be so clearly directed that they will desire the same for their children.

What a beautiful response! As our hearts are connected with the triune God, it is a natural impulse of parents to want the same for their children. Because let's not forget: we are all being discipled into something. If our kids are not being discipled by us into the way of Jesus, they will be discipled by culture into the way of culture. One of these ways leads to death, and the other to life. It is our privilege to direct our hearts to be so profoundly aligned to the heart of the Father that our hearts also turn to our children.

ALMOST THE END, BUT JUST THE BEGINNING

As we come to the end of this book, I pray that this isn't the end but rather the beginning of your journey to raise a disciple. In a culture that wants to disciple us into frenetic parents in a frenetic society and disciple our children into so many other things, it is my great hope for us all that we continue to focus on the most important thing and disciple our children in the way of Jesus. I want to encourage you (and honestly, myself too) to not be tempted to completely outsource your child's discipleship to others. Instead, you and I can partner with our churches in a way that helps our children's spiritual journeys to flourish.

We will all have times of spiritual wealth and spiritual dryness, but throughout every season, it is integral that we continue to persevere in our spiritual practices and model for our children what following Jesus looks like in real life, even when it is hard. And let's be real: following Jesus *is* hard at times. Sometimes for huge chunks of time. But persevering in the faith is a lesson that won't be lost on our kids. Through every age and stage of our children's lives, and our own lives too, we will make so many mistakes. Sorry, it's true. But one thing that will never be a mistake is looking to Jesus in our every action, in our every word, in our every breath. In doing so, we point our kids to Jesus in a gentle and loving way too.

Each age—nope, wait, I mean each day—is unique in the development of children. Because life doesn't have a pause button, it can feel as if one day our children are infants barely able to hold up their own head, and the next day they are starting school, and the very next they are hitting puberty. Every day is precious. (Blah, I said precious. I sound like my mother. I don't use that word lightly. I really do mean it. These are precious days and years.) In every moment, their lives are being formed as the world continues to change around us. What an opportunity we have to raise disciples.

As the church, we speak about going and making disciples. Jesus made it really clear to his disciples, and us by proxy, that *because* all authority on heaven and on earth has been given to him, we need to "go and make disciples of all the nations, baptizing them in the name of the Father and the Son and the Holy Spirit" (Matthew 28:19). We talk about going to make disciples elsewhere, but we sometimes forget something so important: many of us are lucky enough to have them growing in our very homes. Let's not take that for granted. Take the time to talk about Jesus when you are at home. Talk about Jesus when you are on the road. Talk about Jesus when you are going to bed. Talk about Jesus when you get up in the morning. Be a broken record for Jesus. Show and tell your kids that you really do mean what you say about Christ's love for them. Listen, and I mean *really* listen. Lean in. Hear what's being said and what's not being said. Receive their questions and concerns without judgment, and with sincerity and grace. Pray for your child without ceasing. Build the strongest foundation you know how, and be prepared to surrender that foundation to your child and the work of the Spirit in your child's life. And know that your child's story, and yours, is not yet complete. God is at work even when we don't see it.

Throughout this Jesus-centered parenting journey, I pray that each day my heart and yours would be aligned to the heart of the Father. I pray that our kids would follow us as we follow Christ. I pray that we would overflow with the fruit of the Spirit, and that our children would see and know that Christ is at work in us. I pray that our children experience the transformation of Christ through the Spirit. I pray that God would help each of us as we stumble through our very best attempts at raising disciples. May God's will be done in our families as it is in heaven. Amen. Let it be so.

RESOURCES

BIBLES

Infant through age 1

    My First Bible Words (Nashville: Thomas Nelson, 2016)

Ages 1–2

    Frolic First Bible, J. A. Reisch, illustrator (Minneapolis: Sparkhouse Family, 2016)

Ages 1–3

    Pray and Play Bible for Young Children (Loveland, CO: Group Publishing, 1997)

Ages 2–3

    The Rhyme Bible Storybook, L. J. Sattgast and Laurence Cleyet-Merle (Nashville: Zonderkidz, 2012)

Ages 3–7

    The Tiny Truths Illustrated Bible, Joanna Rivard and Tim Penner (Nashville: Zonderkidz, 2019)

Ages 4–8

God's Story 365 (Big Little Studios, 2016)

Ages 6–9

Shine On: A Story Bible (Harrisonburg, VA: Herald Press, 2014)

Ages 6–10

NIrV, The Books of the Bible for Kids, 4 vols. (Nashville: Zonderkidz, 2017)

Ages 7–12

NIrV Study Bible for Kids (Nashville: Zonderkidz, 2015)

Ages 8–12

NIV Kids' Visual Study Bible (Nashville: Zonderkidz, 2017)

Ages 13 and up

Jesus-Centered Bible (Loveland, CO: Group Publishing, 2015)

DEVOTIONALS

Indescribable: 100 Devotions about God and Science, Louie Giglio and Nicola Anderson, illustrator (Nashville: Thomas Nelson, 2017)

The Jesus Creed for Students: Loving God, Loving Others, Scot McKnight with Chris Folmsbee and Syler Thomas (Brewster, MA: Paraclete Press, 2011)

Love Does for Kids, Bob Goff and Lindsey Goff Viducich (Nashville: Thomas Nelson, 2018)

Our Daily Bread for Kids: 365 Meaningful Moments with God, Crystal Bowman, Teri McKinley, and Luke Flowers, illustrator (Grand Rapids, MI: Discovery House, 2014)

Sharing God's Love: The Jesus Creed for Children, Scot McKnight and Laura McKnight Barringer (Brewster, MA: Paraclete Press, 2014)

STORYBOOKS

The Chronicles of Narnia series, C. S. Lewis (New York: HarperCollins)

God's Great Love for You, Rick Warren and Chris Saunders, illustrator (Nashville: Zonderkidz, 2017)

God's Very Good Idea: A True Story of God's Delightfully Different Family, Trillia Newbell and Catalina Echeverri, illustrator (Charlotte, NC: The Good Book Company, 2017)

It Will Be Okay: Trusting God through Fear and Change, Lysa TerKeurst (Nashville: Thomas Nelson, 2014)

Jesus Showed Us!, Brad Jersak and Shari-Anne Vis, illustrator (Brad Jersak, 2016)

When God Made Light, Matthew Paul Turner and David Catrow, illustrator (Colorado Springs: WaterBrook, 2018)

When God Made You, Matthew Paul Turner and David Catrow, illustrator (Colorado Springs: WaterBrook, 2017)

ACKNOWLEDGMENTS

I can't help but feel that this book has been another child I've given birth to (of course, not one as wonderful as my biological child!). And when you give birth, once all the excitement of the delivery is over, you are immensely thankful. I am thankful for the midwifery ways of my editor, Valerie Weaver-Zercher, who helped me bring this baby into the world with grace and excellence. Valerie, you are a beautiful soul, and I have no doubt that the disciples you are raising know your love and the love of Christ in the most wonderful of ways.

Next, even though he probably got scratched and hit and sworn at (all metaphorically, of course!) through this birthing process, I am so thankful for my husband, Sam. Sam, you have partnered with me and taught me methods to disciple that have formed me and our daughter in beautiful ways. I am thankful to be your partner in life, in parenting, and in fun. I love you.

Erin Penny: Kid, you may not fully realize it, but you helped me write a lot of this book. So thanks. You may read this someday and feel that you've been a guinea pig, but I want you to know that all of this is because your dad and I want you to know the deepest love of all: the love of Jesus. I am so thankful that you are my kid and that you are God's kid too. For the rest of your life, I want you to know: you are known, you are loved, and you are enough. Follow Jesus and remember to breathe.

Mom and Dad, thank you for your discipleship: Mom, into the way of Jesus, and Dad, into the way of sport. I appreciate both. Thank you for everything you have done throughout my entire life. I cannot put to words the depth of my appreciation.

Nic and Josh, my brothers: thank you for your support through the writing process. We have had quite the journey together our whole lives through, and I can't imagine all of that without you both. Thank you for teaching me to climb imaginary walls, be an American Gladiator, and shoot hoops so we didn't ruin the garden.

To my wonderful team of prereaders and encouragers who gave me feedback and tough love when I needed it: Ali, Amanda, Anita, Char, Christine, Diane, Janet, Jill, Lynda, Nic, Nina, Sandra, Simon. And to the rest of my home church family, friends, and coworkers at The Meeting House: thank you.

I am thankful that God implanted the desire in my heart to be an author when I was young and continued to cultivate and nurture that desire as I grew older. I am thankful that God has directed my paths throughout my life and opened the door to this book. I am constantly humbled by the way that God is willing to use even me.

NOTES

FOREWORD

1. Scotty Smith, *Everyday Parenting: 365 Days to a Gospel-Centered Faith* (Grand Rapids, MI: Baker Books, 2011), 25.

CHAPTER 1

1. Jessica LaGrone, foreword to *Grow at Home: A Beginner's Guide to Family Discipleship*, by Winfield Bevins (Franklin, TN: Seedbed Publishing, 2016).
2. Lisa Miller, *The Spiritual Child: The New Science on Parenting for Health and Lifelong Thriving* (New York: St. Martin's Press, 2015), 31.

CHAPTER 2

1. Arnold Thackray and David C. Brock, *Moore's Law: The Life of Gordon Moore, Silicon Valley's Quiet Revolutionary* (Philadelphia: Basic Books, 2015), xx.
2. David E. Fitch, *Faithful Presence: Seven Disciplines That Shape the Church for Mission* (Downers Grove, IL: InterVarsity Press, 2016), 133.
3. Vicky Rideout, *The Common Sense Census: Media Use by Tweens and Teens*, ed. Seeta Pai (San Francisco: Common Sense Media, 2015), 59, https://www.commonsensemedia.org/sites/default/files/uploads/research/census_researchreport.pdf.

4. Vicky Rideout, *The Common Sense Census: Media Use by Kids Age Zero to Eight*, ed. Michael B. Robb (San Francisco: Common Sense Media, 2017), 3, http://cdn.cnn.com/cnn/2017/images/11/07/csm_zerotoeight_full.report.final.2017.pdf.

5. Rideout, *The Common Sense Census: Media Use by Tweens and Teens*, 13.

6. Ibid.

CHAPTER 3

1. Anne Boylan, *Sunday School: The Formation of an American Institution, 1790–1880* (New Haven: Yale University, 1988).

2. Dave Wright, "A Brief History of Youth Ministry," The Gospel Coalition, April 2, 2012, https://www.thegospelcoalition.org/article/a-brief-history-of-youth-ministry/.

3. "Parents and Churches Can Help Teens Stay in Church," LifeWay Research, August 7, 2007, https://lifewayresearch.com/2007/08/07/parents-churches-can-help-teens-stay-in-church/.

CHAPTER 5

1. James Penner et al., *Hemorrhaging Faith: Why and When Canadian Young Adults Are Leaving, Staying and Returning to the Church* (Richmond Hill, ON: EFC Youth and Young Adult Ministry Roundtable, 2011), 23.

2. Ibid.

CHAPTER 8

1. Dorothy Singer and Tracey Revenson, *A Piaget Primer* (New York: Penguin, 1978), 12–26.

2. Erik Erikson and Joan Erikson, *The Life Cycle Complete: Extended Version* (New York: W. W. Norton, 1998), 64.

3. James W. Fowler, *Stages of Faith: The Psychology of Human Development* (New York: Harper Collins, 1995), 121.

4. Ibid., 173.

5. Ibid., 182.

CHAPTER 10

1. Simone A. de Roos, "Young Children's God Concepts: Influences of Attachment and Socialization in a Family and School Context" (paper presentation, REA/APRRE Conference, Denver, CO, November 5, 2004), 5.
2. Rachel Held Evans, *Inspired* (Nashville: Nelson Books, 2018), 219.

CHAPTER 11

1. Gary Thomas, *Sacred Pathways: Discovering Your Soul's Path to God* (Grand Rapids: Zondervan, 1996).

CHAPTER 13

1. Gary Thomas, *Sacred Parenting: How Raising Children Shapes Our Souls* (Grand Rapids: Zondervan: 2004), 26.

CHAPTER 14

1. Rick Hiemstra, Lorianne Duek, and Matthew Blackaby, *Renegotiating Faith: The Delay in Young Adult Identity Formation and What It Means for the Church in Canada* (Toronto: Faith Today Publications, 2018), 13.
2. Ibid.

THE AUTHOR

Natalie Frisk is curriculum pastor at The Meeting House Church in Toronto, Ontario, where she and a team create kids' and youth curricula used by churches worldwide. Frisk is a sought-after speaker on topics of youth and children's ministry, spiritual formation, and discipleship. She's a regular guest on the Unseminary podcast, and has been published at the ReKnew and Pangea blogs. Frisk has a master's degree in theological studies from McMaster Divinity College and serves on the board of Be in Christ Church of Canada. She is married to Sam, mom to Erin, and child of God. She loves Jesus, coffee, and samosas.

CPSIA information can be obtained
at www.ICGtesting.com
Printed in the USA
LVHW110111180919
631394LV00001B/2/P